50 USEFUL TIPS ON CHINA
from a guy who ALMOST got it

RALPH JENNINGS

50 Useful Tips on China

By Ralph Jennings

ISBN-13: 978-988-8843-67-1

© 2024 Ralph Jennings

SOCIAL SCIENCE / General

EB204

All rights reserved. No part of this book may be reproduced in material form, by any means, whether graphic, electronic, mechanical or other, including photocopying or information storage, in whole or in part. May not be used to prepare other publications without written permission from the publisher except in the case of brief quotations embodied in critical articles or reviews. For information contact info@earnshawbooks.com

Published in Hong Kong by Earnshaw Books Ltd.

Contents

Introduction — 1

Part I: Life, Self and Self-Image — 5
1. A Little Piece of Happiness — 7
2. When the Jokes Aren't Funny — 12
3. Why It's Always So Noisy in China — 16
4. Sleeping in the Daytime, in Public — 20
5. It's Safer to Think Inside the Box than out — 24
6. When Childhood Ends and How You Can Tell — 29
7. If You Look the Part, You Are the Part — 34
8. Obsession with Seeking Achievement — 38
9. Mixed-use Mania: Anything Goes with Anything — 42
10. The Psychology of Avoiding the Truth — 46
11. Fear of the Ordinary Unknown — 50
12. Eating: Why So Many Things Taste like Well-Done Chicken — 54

Part II: Family and Friends — 59
13. Family as an Economic, Social and Religious Unit — 61
14. Chinese-Foreign Marriages: Is There a Natural Attraction? — 66
15. Who to Impress if Marrying a Chinese Person — 71
16. Shyness Around Strangers if Scolded or Coddled as Children — 76
17. Children Without Siblings Struggle to Find Friends — 80
18. No Favor Ever Forgotten — No Debt Either — 84
19. What the Elderly Look Forward to Most — 88
20. Strangers Are Competitors in Disguise — 92

Part III: School, Work and Money   97

21. Education as Raw Material to Get Rich   99
22. Why English Mastery is Tough Despite Years of Formal Study   103
23. Why Hands Don't Get Raised at Meetings   108
24. Why A-Plus University Students Miss China's Best Jobs   113
25. Dreams, Decisions and Demons that Divide Them   117
26. Money Handlers, Not Shopkeepers   121
27. Big Brother, Little Sister: Workplace Relations   126
28. Everyone Wants to Be the Boss and Here's How They Do It   130
29. Why Employees Work Overtime, Even When the Work is Done   135
30. Why It's Acceptable to Copy Without Permission   139
31. Almost Is Good Enough   144
32. What's Up with Gambling, from Macau to the Financial Markets?   149
33. Never Pay Full Price—There's Always Another Way   154
34. The Customer Is Always Right, as Long as the Company Agrees   159

Part IV: Chinese Society and the World   165

35. Curiosity and How it Helps the Chinese   167
36. When a Smiling Face is Hiding Hostility   172
37. Why You Get Someone to Guide You Everywhere   177
38. When to Donate to Charity   181
39. A Law in Heaven and a Method on Earth   185
40. New or Old? One Right Answer   190
41. Medication: Anything Will Do if You Believe in It   195
42. What Chinese Think of Foreigners and How Foreigners Can Adapt   200

43.	Shoving, Spitting, Staring and Driving	205
44.	Non-Violence as a Strict Code for Handling Disputes	209
45.	Policing Where Law Is Third Priority	213
46.	Why a Chinese Person Makes the Perfect Dinner Date	218
47.	Why Superstition Has an Outsized Following	223
48.	Why Authorities Get Blamed for Just About Everything	228
49.	Nature: Conquer It or Get Conquered	232
50.	Quiz for Foreigners: Are You a Good Fit in China?	237

Epilogue: The Chinese Tea Taste Test   244

About the Author   249

INTRODUCTION

You're traveling to Beijing with your fiancé who was born in China. Years later, your employer says go to the homeland of the scholar Confucius and write a report about the 21st Century investment climate. Suppose you never go to China but have Chinese classmates at your university at home and later Chinese co-workers. Or maybe you just read every day about the Sino-US trade war, the Covid-19 aftermath and Chinese President Xi Jinping's designs to expand his 1.4-billion-person country's economic influence abroad.

China is said, just as Russia once was, to be a riddle wrapped in a mystery inside an enigma. For the outsider peeking in, many aspects of Chinese society can be confusing, unusual and surprising, but every one of them has its logic. Why, for example, do foreigners usually get stared at in public? How do a lot of Chinese 12-year-olds endure thirteen hours of classroom learning every day and still get up the next morning?

In the chapters ahead, I will take you on my passage through China, which, in fact, included a trip to the area where the venerated scholar Confucius grew up.

50 Useful Tips on China, from a Guy who Almost Got It is more than a description of Chinese ideas, customs and cultural highlights. This book takes fifty typical patterns of thought or behavior — those most likely to confuse, bemuse and delight someone who's new to it all — and explores the underlying reasons for each one. By knowing why some people stare, gamble and seek their parents' approval for marriage, for example, you will be more likely to treat people in China with understanding and compassion. You will at least understand what's up, making it easier to choose the right words and pursue fruitful interactions with locals, from picking a lunch date to penning an important business deal. An outsider's relations with Chinese people, as with any culture in the world, vastly improve through simply getting to know them.

During my anthropology studies at UC Berkeley, I fell for the reductive, functionalist approach to analyzing a society: everything has a matter-of-factual reason that can be understood if broken down and analyzed from the base elements upward. The Chinese way of doing things, as that anywhere else, is neither random nor mysterious. It has been shaped over decades and centuries as ordinary people respond to tangible, external factors. Three decades of news reporting, including more than two of those in greater China, have made this functionalist search for truth a daily thing for me.

The underlying causes I found most often for the different cultural or social practices cited in the pages ahead trace back to poverty, scarcity of resources in a crowded country and a deep-seated belief that the best way to organize all social arrangements and human interactions is hierarchy including that within a vibrant, resilient extended family. Chinese, at the same time, are always trying to catalogue things going on around them, in their minds, to bring order to the fast-changing and often opaque society. There is a yearning for order that explains many social codes such as the deeply rooted respect for paternalistic authoritarian management at all levels, including in the family. Resource scarcity, low incomes and an aloof style of leadership have taught people to rely heavily on social relationships to get ahead. Those factors help to explain why strangers are usually viewed as competitors rather than potential collaborators and attitudes toward education and childcare reflect these nationwide conditions. Many of the trends span multiple phases of Chinese history rather than just a single dynasty or the communist era of today.

In China, as anywhere, one generation passes its credo to the next, which does the same to the following generation in a more diluted form. That means that even if a family no longer lives in poverty, the young adults will still be influenced by ideas and actions used generations ago to survive with scarce resources. Inter-generational teachings have special weight in China because the country is, to a remarkable extent, culturally insulated from the outside world, which tends to be viewed as a source of competing ideas.

The term 'Chinese', for this book's purposes, applies primarily to ethnic Han citizens of the giant nation of China, but many of the cases made here apply just as well to ethnic Chinese people living in other parts of the world.

50 Pieces of Advice on China, from a Guy who Almost Got It does not actively seek to compare China with other countries, although it is written with the curious outsider in mind. A lot of the analysis here also applies to other places, particularly in East Asia, whose cultures and historical events are intertwined with China. However, this book stresses characteristics that are rigorously, intensely Chinese. For example, construction projects are hanging from urban skylines all over Asia, but the Chinese have demolished, built and refurbished their structures with a speed and fervor that far exceeds those of any of their neighbors.

Understandably, no part of this book applies to everyone in the wildly diverse country that is China. For every habit and state of mind outlined in the chapters ahead, at least tens of millions or more think and act differently. It's best to see each idea in the book as a prevailing wind rather than a fixed rule.

So why am I the right tour guide? I've reported news and taught newswriting in China, giving me more than the average foreigner's exposure to common people. I once spent five to ten hours a week yakking with local people in teahouses and in Sichuan-style restaurants about topics of their choice. A weekly advice column that I wrote for a Beijing newspaper for about seven years brought letters from Chinese people annoyed by their university courses or mad at their parents, to name just two recurring themes. The letters left me a clear sense of the struggles affecting youth. I spent some of my greater China years in Taiwan and Hong Kong where I met lots more insightful people as a reporter and university instructor.

But back to the riddle and the enigma, I still get baffled by China. So, on the journey ahead, learn and laugh and even lament with me over the findings. Join my tour against the big scenic backdrop of knowing one thing: I may not know what I'm talking about.

Part I
Life, Self and Self-Image

A Little Piece of Happiness

Dead-end, even dangerous jobs justify the wages they bring in. Too often, the point of university study is to learn a skill that generates money rather than to learn more about a field of genuine, organic personal interest. Such work-life sacrifices are very common in China because a lot of people are seeking what a Chinese cliché calls 'a little piece of happiness'.

That little piece, to put it bluntly, is money for the family. A little means a lot for a people who are historically used to poverty and social chaos, two factors that can make obtaining life's basics difficult. Both help to explain why so many Chinese make glaring personal quality-of-life sacrifices to earn only a mediocre increase in income. This trade-off happens all over the world, especially where poverty has weighed on a sizable swathe of the population, but it stands out in China because of a socio-politically volatile 20th Century and competition driven by a large population.

China was at war in the 1930s and 1940s, and then poverty continued to grip people throughout the 1950s. Famine hit parts of the country a decade later, and the Cultural Revolution in the 1960s and 1970s resulted in more chaos and destruction. But

China's population hit a breakneck growth streak after 1960, a contributor to many types of scarcity. The 1.4 billion people in China today stress not food, but education and well-paid career jobs.

Things are better now than fifty years ago in so many ways, but the memories of poverty, chaos and their attendant dangers linger in the collective memory. A lot of elders who remember the Cultural Revolution wonder whether China will ever be shaken again in such a way.

Plenty of people in China today also wonder what the government will do next with the economy, especially making changes that could impact directly on their lives, such as sudden new rules for the property and capital markets. Both investments represent wealth within reach, but there is always the question of what position is being taken by the 'central government'.

The typical answer to these doubts: capture as soon as possible at almost any expense enough income to ensure a serviceable home, a family in good health and no immediate threat of having it all suddenly upended.

The common tales of China's migrant workers tell the most gripping stories of sacrifice because, despite the country's efforts and recent improvements, much of rural China remains relatively poor.

Working-age people in rural China, a hub of gritty and low-paid work linked to agriculture, earn money away from home for years because of the higher economic rewards. For instance, on average, they can earn more rushing red-hot plates of food from a kitchen to elite customers in Shanghai or laying bricks all night on a windy, dusty construction project in Beijing. Urban labor pays easily more than $400 per month, up from rural wages averaging closer to $275.

I knew a teahouse server in Beijing who seldom had time

or money to visit her hometown just three hours away by train. Her parents agonised and understood at the same time. Migrants in the cities might live with co-workers in ex-urban shacks and temporary prefabs that have poor heating and no air conditioning. They deem that sacrifice worth it. I remember too the pride of a Shanxi Province cave-dwelling couple whose son was back from a city for a holiday with enough money at least to buy everyone a round of hard candies. Normally the family survives on farming tiny steep plots in the arid hills near their cave.

Reunited with family often only once a year for the Lunar New Year holiday, city-based migrants embrace their once-tiny children who, after an emotional goodbye, had grown dramatically in their absence. Now the child is more distant, the ward of textbooks, exams and extra-curricular classes. But that's fine with the parents. They see study as a route to high scores on the national university entrance exam and, after the university years, a gateway to workplaces bringing more income than fields, kitchens and construction sites.

The returned migrant workers bring with them their money from the city. Their children, parents and probably other relatives will spend it on several little pieces of happiness: aircon, refrigerators, a child's education and maybe even a home entertainment system. These gains show bold progress beyond the ravages of the past. It is for that reason families with migrant workers tend to tolerate the sadness, the awkwardness of parents and grown children working in a city that's a 24-hour train ride from home.

They are not alone in making these sacrifices. Tens of millions of urban natives, driven by their parents' desire for financial security, sacrifice their real ambitions by tolerating dull desk jobs that pay steadily rather than taking riskier yet more interesting work in startups, leisure and the arts. Every week, it seemed, someone would write to my newspaper column about hating a job but loving the stable income. Many of them had already slogged through university majors, particularly the hard sciences that offered great financial rewards but were of no personal interest. They aced exams to stand out as job applicants, however, they tended to have no real passion for science. I'd get column letters asking whether there was still a chance to dive into a career in the arts, move to France or both.

Answer: usually no. The inter-generational pressures would instead dictate that in case of any financial trouble, one person's income is potential income for the whole family.

Something else that's not easy but is widely done to lock in money is using even the most tenuous of personal connections to get ahead. People, under pressure from parents, often seek to marry people who are financially better off, and moving up the happiness scale is viewed very much in material terms. People who have cemented the basics for themselves pursue the same for their adult children (university tuition looms large), aging parents and increasingly distant relatives. Family unity, such as bringing migrants back together with geographically distant spouses, comes further down the list.

If China follows the trend of more developed countries as prosperity levels rise, eventually the population is going to sigh with exhaustion and seek relief. Sacrifices will taper off and people will shun needless ambition, instead drawing inward to focus on neglected heart-and-soul stuff, such as family togetherness, and zeroing in on the higher levels of physical comfort, even if just replacing wooden stools with armchairs. They will seek knowledge because they like knowing things, not just using it as a way to get jobs.

In Taiwan, a prism through which China's Mainland future

can sometimes be understood, tough farming and fishing work once underpinned the economy. Citizens would migrate far from home to make money and grease connections for work even when it hurt to ask. Industrialization in the 1980s allowed most people a comfortable lifestyle and although elders remember being poor and pass their anxieties on to the next generation, many young people nowadays spend lavish amounts of time with family—even if they could earn more away—and on their own pastimes. Adults who live away from family do it as much for adventure as for income.

Younger people in China already want a greater amount of happiness in their life. Increasing numbers are keen on sports, adventure and hanging out. I met a few punk rockers and serial leisure travelers in Beijing who didn't fight with their parents as they might in a more hardscrabble part of China. They had this this option only because their elders had sacrificed previously for the family's initial 'little piece of happiness'.

When the Jokes Aren't Funny

What's funny in China doesn't always set off laughter in other countries. A Westerner trying to liven up a quiet dinner party in China could easily find the Chinese guests all the deader by making jokes about sex, marriage or oneself, for example. Or, from parties I recall, people could laugh just because I'm laughing, to appear in sync and not offend me. Colorful slams against classes of people or institutions, such as the long list of 'blonde' jokes famous in my homeland, the United States, don't garner much attention either. How many so-and-sos does it take to change a light bulb? Any answer more than one or two would befuddle many in an average Chinese audience. On the flip side, Chinese people at a dinner party can laugh the house down at jokes that would puzzle a foreigner. Chinese humor usually relies on getting the subtle, double meanings of individual words plus the depth of cliches and references to people and institutions that are uniquely Chinese. Smarmy deadpan humor has a following in China much as it does in other countries.

Getting the joke requires an understanding of its uniquely Chinese origins, I found after routinely missing punchlines for years but daring to ask friends "so what was so funny?". The humor value usually revolves first around saving face for the joke teller and the people about whom he cares. Topics of jokes correlate closely to what Chinese people understand the best. Wisecracks about China's elaborate, often excessive and widely known drinking culture among the rich and powerful get the guffaws going among groups of middle-class people. Quips that emerge from a racially diverse society, usually targeted at a particular race including one's own, have no currency in China where 90-plus percent of people have basically the same racial makeup. Humor rooted in irony or satire celebrates the richness of double meanings in the Chinese language. Appreciation for deadpan reflects a can't-do-anything-about-it view of society's endless roster of daily life difficulties and contradictions.

And here's something I never expected: a 2013 study called 'Sense of humor in China: the role of individualism, collectivism and face work' says Asians, including Chinese, make jokes to give or to save face. That means jokes against certain people or oneself violate the saving of face. It makes sense that jokes related to drinking would work as those quips give face to collective activity—a celebrated but still sort of gee-whizzy facet of the middle-class lifestyle—while offending no one in particular.

Reliance on wording nuances underscores the depth and particularities of the Chinese language. Chinese has thrived for centuries on a dictionary's worth of set four-word phrases or sayings, terse metered poems and rampant double entendre. Here's a classic poem-slash-joke from one of my own Chinese-language books, *China Jokes & Behaves*:

Wheels spin in the morning
Plates spin at noon
Dice spin in the afternoon
Skirts spin at night.

The Chinese word for 'spin' (轉) can mean roll, rotate, turn, twirl and other things that might better fit the translation here. But clearly the poet is using this single versatile word plus China's tradition of short poems to mock with humor the habits of officials who eat lavish lunches just after getting to work, gamble afterwards and look for prostitutes once off work. Told at a dinner party of private sector working people, this joke would make everyone laugh. It reinforces bonds among ordinary people who lack the privileges of cushy jobs. In fact, the poet, if pressed, could argue his lines have nothing to do with public officials. No individual people or types of people are expressly named.

Enthusiasm for deadpan jokes, a hallmark of dark humor, arises from the opacity of Chinese society. Opacity covers money scams, graft and a government that thrives on telling its citizens that all's well despite contradictory signs. It's hard to read newspapers every day lauding the construction of a 'harmonious society', to use a common phrase from officialdom, yet hear about various scams from one's own personal network without rolling the eyes. A joke I picked up in 2021 goes like this: if you don't upgrade to an iPhone 12 today, you'll save about US$1,000. Then when you actually do buy an iPhone 12, because of the money saved today, you'll feel like it's free.

Adding language flexibility to deadpan, Chinese netizens came up with the term 'grass mud horse' (third tone 'cao', second tone 'ni', and third tone 'ma') as a proxy for one of the language's most profane phrases and a way of protesting internet censorship. It's funny because some netizens have posted ironic images and videos of what a 'grass mud horse' looks like—a white shaggy llama that's endearing enough to be someone's pet.

As for why foreign humor often doesn't strike at Chinese laughter nerves, China can still be tough place to live, and a lot of people see everything at their disposal as a tool for getting ahead somehow, be that a duck they can de-feather and sell or a wad of clay they can mold into a drinking cup. This intensely practical view of one's surroundings hardly casts the world as a place lending itself to jokes about light bulbs. Why waste time or energy or the light bulb itself or mess around with different ways to screw it into a socket?

Toilet humor and sex jokes, I found, hardly crack a grin in a country where men still undress in front of strangers in stall-free restrooms. This brand of humor thrives in the West, I'm guessing, largely on the secrecy surrounding the topic of nudity against a Protestant ethic. Without the religious-based taboos, the jokes don't work so well. There's nothing deadpan about it. It gives no one face, and it sure won't excite people at a dinner party.

Why It's Always So Noisy in China

China operates at a high volume. Elevator chatter can reach the same volume as fans belting out cheers and taunts at sporting events anywhere in the world. Whoops and peals of laughter fill Chinese noodle diners, likewise at football matches peppered with 'Beijing profanity' so extreme that local officials have urged fans to cool it. Families raise their voices in excitement when they visit parks, prompting quieter visitors to boost their own so they can be heard. Trucks rumble through the streets after midnight to offload iron scaffolding bars for construction work. Their idling engines send a humming vibration through people's windows, and steel bars slamming onto the hard pavement adds percussion to the bass. Buildings of all types explode with hammer-and-drill remodeling projects from 7:00 a.m. to as late as 10:00 p.m. Jackhammers join the chorus outdoors by blasting apart old cement buildings for eventual redevelopment, which itself is a noisy multiyear endeavor. Fireworks dominate the extended Lunar New Year season over three to four weeks.

There are peers abroad, to be sure. Americans have a reputation for being loud talkers. Heavy metal concerts in the West are known as walls of noise. Crowds in the average Irish bar in San

Francisco gab so loudly that patrons seeking deep conversation step outside. But noise is the norm in China because lots of people don't feel fazed by it. The country is densely populated. The people are used to noise. They even find it energizing. When it's their turn to ramp up the volume, say for home remodeling, they figure no one will protest, which is generally true.

Chinese cities are densely populated by international norms, so many a sound made by one person inevitably lands in the ears of others who didn't necessarily want to hear it. Because so many people grow up in the crossfire of sharp, blaring external sounds, they become acclimated. Citizens of more sparsely populated countries often grow up in detached houses on quiet streets with just the odd passing car and barking dog, so a demolition project next door would obviously jolt their peace. Due to migration from the sparsely populated countryside into the cities, multi-family apartment compounds house most people in China today. Newer, urban compounds are typically riddled with the hammering and drilling of remodeling projects plus the neighbors stomping around upstairs. The same goes for offices.

When I worked as a copy editor at the state-run newspaper *China Daily*, the management thought modernization meant a spiffier office building. *China Daily* brought in crews to hammer and drill for months as we edited stories in the next room. There was no consideration of moving us offsite until the polished white walls, wooden floors and lobby fountain were done. Hundreds of colleagues and I just listened to the atomic farting of drills as we worked. Everyone but me and a few other Westerners was used to a noisy environment.

Some people complain. But far more often they just get on with it: *China Daily* never missed a day of publication during the projects. People in other occupations easily rise after noisy nights to take math tests, design websites and make sales calls, for example, as their noisy next day roars into force.

If still perturbed, most people just throw up a hand with the comment *mei banfa*, which means "there's no way around it." They can't imagine stopping a construction project, for example, and they're usually right.

It's just a short cry from acclimation to appreciation of noise. Loud building construction rings of national progress rather than disruption, because new buildings and public infrastructure exude prosperity and Chinese officials have long told their people that the two are intertwined. Chinese hope their country's development level will rise to that of Western countries. As more proof that noise is fun, curb side events, including even the most brazen of marketing ploys, quickly draw excited crowds. The marketers in charge thrash drums and scream through microphones and amplifiers.

Silence is an eerie alternative. Elders might associate a quiet home with the lonely absence of children. The superstitious among them equate quiet spaces with the threat of ghosts. As a growing contingent of younger Chinese people tires of fireworks as a must-have Lunar New Year tradition, old-timers complain that the holiday just doesn't have the 'atmosphere' that it once did. In large open offices, employees often equate prolonged silences with tension on the job, opposite to the warmth that would spawn chatter and laughter.

Company parties in China normally revolve around raucous raffles and singing contests because noise beats silence. Quiet events would pressure invitees to converse, a burden on company employees, many of whom are just there because a no-show would look bad. Centralised events nullify the need for conversation.

No formula fits all in China, of course. Liu Anjun of Beijing explained to me in 2005 what happens to a complainer. I met the older man through a friend one day and he told me police were on his case. Officers had tired of his complaining about the noise from a construction project near his home. Nothing changed at the construction site, so the law tried to fix Mr Liu. He eventually did jail time for protesting.

A lot of hotels double pane their windows against any late-night trucks and close the karaoke lounge at 11:00 p.m. so guests can sleep. Hotel clerks offer room changes to people annoyed by on-site remodeling so they're further away from the sound. Plenty of park goers sit in peace playing chess and drinking tea.

And China keeps changing. More people line up in public now than ever, for example, and awareness of consumer rights has surged since an outbreak of food safety issues in 2008. Noise is becoming a new target of this trend. I saw a report on China's *Global Times* website on audio disturbances in the mega city of Shanghai in 2014. Apartment renovation led the list of complaints, followed by traffic and groups of women who dance outdoors to the sound of boom boxes. Families sometimes lose so much patience that they move, temporarily or for good, out of their noisy apartments. But most people put up with it and stay. Police or building managers generally regard noise disputes as too sundry to warrant their time. I tried it in one Beijing apartment, got two officers to take a report and made the building manager promise to enforce weekend-quiet rules. Then the guy upstairs just kept drilling seven days a week.

Why gripe at all? Most people are too steeled against loud noise to mind it. It might even sound like music.

Sleeping in the Daytime, in Public

A noticeable number of bus passengers in China zonk out on rides of more than a few minutes. Every second or third person in a university library is asleep and anyone who teaches a class will see students fold their arms over their desks and put their heads down. I got so tired of lecturing to people's hair, rested in their folded arms, that I imposed a no-sleeping rule in my most recent classes and enshrined it on the course introduction slides. Older adults often nod off during conferences and lectures, although of course most people do stay awake. No small number of university instructors with students from multiple countries laud Chinese classmates as their most attentive, and China wouldn't enjoy today's economic advances if everyone was sleeping on the job. But the number of people who sleep by day, in public spaces, is enough to generate a caffed-up internet debate about what's going on.

So, finally I used my journalist's privileges over a few days to interview sleep experts in greater China and see whether they could crack that debate. They told me spotty night-time sleep and the lifelong customs of taking naps in China, long past the primary school years, explain the prevalence of shuteye when the sun is shining.

They explained noise and light are common at night in many Chinese homes, challenging even heavy sleepers. That's usually because relatives unwittingly keep children awake. A seven-year-old might wait up every night for a parent to come home from late shifts to avoid sleeping alone, meaning she doesn't sleep until 10:00 p.m. or 11:00 p.m. despite an early rise the next day for elementary school. I saw one cross-cultural sleep research paper saying just four percent of children in Asia fall asleep on their own, versus with a parent in the room. Parents in China feel safest with their children beside them at night in case things go wrong. Children get comfortably used to co-sleeping.

Multiple people over three generations often sleep in a single room, giving everyone a sense of intimacy and safety. Children typically need two or three more hours of sleep per night than their elders, so after a child drifts off, adults in the room will watch television or pace around organising things. Hours later, adults rise before the child gets up to prepare for going to work. Adults keep one another awake too. Even if some are technically sleeping, the sounds of those still awake jolt them out of their sleep for countless thirty-second intervals during the night.

Neighbors in dense apartment complexes further threaten sleep. Karaoke bars in mixed-use buildings send bass vibrations and singers' howls through walls. Some of the residents with night shifts and active singles' lifestyles slam doors and clomp across floors throughout the night, all audible to their neighbors. Sound-proof construction materials would cost so much that developers often don't bother with them. No one expects it, anyway. Per Chapter 3, noise is as integral to everyday life as rice and tea.

Outside apartment complexes, motor scooters, railway lines, convenience stores, night clubs and 24-hour construction sites can further deplete sleep. Cities in China usually lack the sort of serious zoning enforcement that would require physical distance between homes and, say, bar districts. Anyone who goes to bed after a night shift in China risks waking three to four hours later to hammer blows and drilling work from remodeling in nearby apartments. I got stuck in that timing trap during my first year in China, when I worked copy-editing shifts until around midnight and got to bed a couple hours later. Remodeling normally starts up around 8:00 a.m. In my case it was just one thin floor away.

Increasing numbers of people live in this dense, mixed-use ecosystem because of China's urbanization. Smaller towns are quieter, the houses often single-family, but the cities offer more material comforts and better job prospects.

I couldn't help noticing that Elizabeth Pantley's venerable childcare book, *The No-Cry Sleep Solution for Toddlers and Preschoolers,* says people—of all ages—sleep best when it's quiet. That means even one's spouse rummaging through a drawer in the bedroom past midnight can wake the other half. Enough disruptions at night stop people from delving long enough into a deep slumber to let the body and brain recover for the next day. That next day, the body needs rest and finds the easiest way to get it: a nap outside the home.

Chinese kindergartens, like those in much of the world, make naptime a formal part of the daily routine. Teachers lay down their children after lunch. Chinese elementary schools extend the routine by sending children home for a half-hour nap. Sleep isn't always an elective. Some teachers inspect each head and sometimes scold those who remain alert. Eventually just about everyone acclimates—and not just throughout childhood.

Because so many people are used to napping, plenty of workplaces allow or encourage naps during the lunch hour. Hardly anyone protests. Lunch happens to be a full-course meal for most people in China, too, not a vending machine sandwich. Chinese commonly say such a load in the stomach adds to their urge to sleep. China happens to lack the violent crime common in much of the West, so people can sleep in public with little concern about a mugging or even a pickpocketing. Adults with low-stress jobs may nap for thirty to sixty minutes a day.

Widespread napping among adults sets China apart from much of the world outside Asia, occasionally irritating outsiders. At a foreign media office where I worked, to cite one example, one senior reporter would throw his shoulders back in a tall ergonomic desk chair and close his eyes for ten or fifteen minutes after lunch. He had young children and sleeping all night was often impossible. His foreign-born supervisor resented the naps and asked the reporter to stay awake in case of breaking news. Disrupted nighttime sleep plus a lifelong habit of naps had made daytime dozing so acceptable that it took a boss's order to stop it.

It's Better to Think Insde the Box than Out

Think outside the box, teachers and tech company bosses admonish their charges in the West. Less so in China. More than a few Chinese phone receptionists glibly tell callers that so-and-so isn't around without jumping out of their box to take a message, suggest a call-back time or offer another number. As a journalist calling people for information, I usually ask on my own whether I can leave a message. Sticking with my trade, a lot of Chinese reporters work more comfortably as note takers than people hired to synthesize their notes and field observations into unique stories. I've met academic researchers who believe they're writing quality papers by summarizing old publications rather than creating new material based on their own surveys or experiments. They're thinking in a box.

Confucianism, a code of moral and social conduct that surged in popularity around 140 AD to ensure stability, reveals the key reason so many people 'think in the box' today. Confucianism encourages each person to accept a fixed place in society. Society in turn progresses because everyone knows what to do instead of feeling unclear about the expectations of oneself and others. A farmer, for example, should plow land, sell cabbage and behave in a way typically expected of farmers. They shouldn't sell real estate for part of the day even if those activities don't hurt anyone. That would just be confusing for all.

China remains a fractious, often opaque country where people largely live in grey zones. It's unclear in modern China, for instance, who is senior to whom in a lot of workplaces or whether it's okay to sell food from certain curb sides without a permit. In-the-box thinking allows people to seek orderly relief from this daily ambiguity. Confucianism is still popular, consciously or unconsciously.

The in-the-box ethic starts early. A lot of teachers from elementary school onward encourage students to write essays by copying from books and, at the end, inserting a quick line of opinion — often the piece's only stamp of originality. The students don't learn to write papers that would reflect their own analysis from top to bottom, using book passages only to support their ideas.

In business, Chinese smartphone developers dominate offshore peers in the number of handsets sold around the world. But a lot of successful tech firms succeed less because of raw invention than on account of me-too technology, competitive prices and the vast domestic market size. Me-too is classic boxed thinking. Chinese brand Xiaomi's first smartphones were described precisely as iPhone lookalikes that sold for less than half the price of an iPhone. I ran into a *Harvard Business Review* piece a few years back that put this entrepreneurial spirit about as bluntly as possible: "outside the country (China), most of its businesspeople are better known for amassing wealth than for innovative management ideas."

Among the most intriguing 'boxes' are those that demarcate social relations. Many Chinese label their friendships and other voluntary associations to explain to anyone involved or inquiring from outside why they have these relationships. Obvious roles are business partner, supplier, teacher, student and work colleague — even if the relationship rests more on going out for tea and a chat than the transactions implied by these labels. A friend who is more than five years older gets called 'older brother' or 'teacher' to give reason and order to the relationship.

Foreigners in China wear their own special labels in social settings.

I wear several badges when meeting people in China to hang out. They're assigned based on my age and any role expectations, sometimes with the adjective 'foreign' tacked on. I get called 'teacher', for example, if I'm older than a friend. I know what the badge says when my friends talk to other local people about me. That means the label a friend uses matters most to the outside world. It's a confirmation of one's place in the social order. I had one friend who was honest with her mother. I was labeled 'friend', which was true, as we had known each other for years as nothing but hang-out buddies. Should she have said "teacher" instead? Her mother asked her not to see me anymore.

The term 'friend' falls into one of those awkward grey zones again. Traditional people looking into someone's friendship may ask: are the two people dating? Is the relationship transactional somehow? If not, isn't it a waste of time? Families are supposed to form such tight social units in China that relatives can provide most of the warm, supportive friendship that anyone needs. Families trend this way for historic lack of trust in outsiders, who might be shady envoys from the opaque world full of competitors, users and backstabbers. No one wants friends like that.

Traditional people seeking pure, non-transactional friendships join groups. A group provides cover. Its members can say something like, "I'm a Rotarian, therefore, I go to weekly

Rotary Club members," instead of trying to explain why they randomly see someone one-on-one in a bar for a drink without a formal reason.

Of course, many Chinese people are inventive. They have ideas for new technology and groundbreaking theses for academic research. They seek out relationships that breach conventional definitions such as 'teacher' and 'business partner.' Entrepreneurs take risks, from cutting prices to leveraging tenuous ties in government to advance their businesses. But the 'in-box' culture of China stops a lot of ideas from taking off.

Conversely, about a million people take the civil service qualifying exam every year but just one in sixty-three takers gets hired. Civil service offers the status of government work with stable pay, a fixed scope of work and low to no odds of getting fired. These posts guarantee order. They are an iron box.

Among the who's who of entrepreneurs, quite a few set up companies because China was poorer during their youth and stable, safe, respectably paid jobs were hard to find. These company founders were trying to pay bills rather than scratch an inner itch to try out a new product they had thought up. Young people now brainstorm ideas for apps that could make money, to name just one type of innovation. But many a risk-averse parent scolds these notions as haughty, dangerously ambitious or just downright dumb. Parents have plenty of sway in China, especially over adult children who live at home and use family income. As a result, inventive, entrepreneurial ideas often die and the brains behind them end up in stable but mindless jobs — soothing parents who crave a Confucian-style order.

Many younger Chinese break out of the social boxes to make friends, too, but again parental scrutiny is often there. Hanging out, Mom and Dad suppose, should be done with a purpose such as building job connections and finding spouses.

50 USEFUL TIPS ON CHINA

To the conservative parent, fun outings among 'just friends' feels opaque, useless and risky. Social roles are hazily defined, defying order. The whole notion is too out of the box.

When Childhood Ends and How You Can Tell

I once met a nine-year-old artist in Beijing. I don't mean she doodled, traced and colored between lines. Her paintings showed in an upmarket, downtown gallery and that's how I met her — a city reporter looking for a gee-whiz story. In her free time she'd paint more and that was about it, aside from the crush of school work. Behind her were two anxious parents fixated on her making it big. Her childhood was over.

Books for toddlers through tweens in China's bookstores are generally aimed, directly or indirectly, at something equally practical — formal education. At a store run by the media giant Xinhua in the southern city Xiamen, I noticed that children as young as three were listed as the target readers of study guides for double-digit addition and subtraction. Tablet PCs with English-instruction software were selling at one point on every floor of the store's five floors. English-language textbooks for extracurricular use dominated an entire level. Chinese classrooms are not necessarily festooned with posters and holiday decorations. All eyes are supposed to be trained on the main attractions: blackboards and teachers. And after the compulsory school day ends, students from many wealthier homes take private, sometimes underground lessons in English, math and computers. In the nine-year-old's case, there was all that plus art.

Children's natural childhood instincts, to play and explore through informal activities, usually get cut off by elementary school. Mom and Dad will have assigned these kids a mission: score better than their peers, however many hours and years the preparation takes. They're being groomed to stay ahead of China's academic competition and eventually land a well-paid job after university graduation with enough money to ensure income for the whole family. Mothers and fathers from this mold probably fear their kids can never start getting ahead too early, lest someone else's kid excels first.

Bookstores in many countries tend to go big on DIY activity booklets and animal stories for their youngest readers. Children in Western countries are encouraged to have fun while learning. They learn through play anyway, as Russian social psychologist Lev Vygotsky has written. His idea helped shape how a lot of Westerners like myself and my own children see early-childhood development. Playtime grew popular outside China because parents believe activities, such as puzzles and the make-believe, teach real world problem-solving skills and situational analysis. Those skills are harder to glean from textbooks. Elementary schools in a lot of countries encourage arts, crafts and dodgeball as well as learning the basics of math and language. Their students get off school by mid-afternoon to focus on something of their choosing—football, for example.

In China, elementary school children attend class for an average of 8.6 hours per day, according to the state-owned *China Daily*. They compete for ranks in their classes through test scores and may be assigned classroom seats in ways that reveal who has got higher scores.

Homework takes another hammer to plenty of childhoods in China. These assignments might take another two hours per evening after the final school bell rings around 4:00 p.m. even though homework is hardly instinctual for most elementary school-aged children. Once home, the average child is tempted instead by toys and, nowadays, mobile phones. The natural urge to be a kid surrounds the child, but undone homework stops temptation. Some kids take the better part of a school year to get used to it.

This chain of events unfolded in front of me when my two daughters got boot-camped into Taipei elementary school with ninety minutes of homework every weekday from about 5:00 p.m. Before starting homework, such as on the walk home from school, their moods would range from somber to jumpy and inattentive. Those shifts reflected dread of the homework, especially harder assignments such as mathematical formulas to compute volumes using *pi*. They learned to hack it within the first few weeks of each school year (and always got play time by late evening courtesy of an American dad).

Pre-teens complete their homework largely to avoid angering their teachers and parents and being scolded in front of classmates. Textbook assignments may offer little sense of achievement except for just getting it all done. For slow or disinterested students, the challenge becomes how to finish fast, leading to corner-cutting and rationales such as, "Who cares if the teacher puts a red X on the question that I missed?" Common complaints: boring, confusing, sore hands from constant writing. Eventually the tough routine becomes a habit. Children, after all, do well with routines. Young brains can be rewired in preparation for many years to follow.

Families who can afford it normally put their children in a

private 'cram school' after their regular school days end, though the Chinese government was discouraging this option as of 2023. The first cram school in China was established by Confucius, placing it at about 500 years B.C. These schools were first used to train future government officials. Today the term refers to an institution that fills children with extra knowledge aimed at helping them to excel in regular school classes. Classes may start only after dinner and last until 9:00 p.m.

After-school classes undoubtedly improve academic performance. And performance breeds scores that determine where children get to study. Institutions that Chinese people call 'key schools' form a coveted minority of the total and some parents look for a backdoor to key school admission if they live outside the geographic district. Key high schools require tough pre-admission exams for incoming middle schoolers. Another daunting standardized exam, the *gaokao*, places the top-scoring high school graduates in China's best universities.

Teachers in China get evaluated based on the average scores of their students, so they often steer their students to get high scores on standardized exams, a pursuit that reduces the chance of teaching, say, sports or musical instruments. A professional English teacher whom I knew from my newspaper Q&A columns once lamented an exam the school suddenly scheduled for her class on a week's notice would decide whether she could advance in her career.

Before exams, some elementary school children who would normally play with dolls or dinosaurs get so nervous they have trouble sleeping, but most children adapt pretty easily to the night-before butterflies. They're already skilled at handling change. The dolls have been literally shelved anyway so that their pre-teen owners can become professional information crammers with no play time. In our home, dolls actually sat on bookshelves and at bedsides cheering the girls on.

Public schools allow two months off for summer break and another month or so for Lunar New Year. Competition-wary parents with the money fill most of that time by sending their children to extra classes that can take up most of the day.

From the parental point of view, China is overpopulated with the best jobs going to a tiny sliver of a huge workforce. They may figure they're on their own, if they fall into poverty or run up a debt, rather look to the state for help (more in Chapter 13). Some have privileged family connections that augur stable, well-paid employment for children after they graduate. The rest basically rely on scores from grade one through college to get a high-paid job. The years of cramming are supposed to help with those scores.

These early years of competition do help children as adults. They're able to vie, assiduously and without getting daunted for too long, for scholarships, well-paid jobs and workplace promotions. Students used to ten to twelve hours of study per day should have little trouble grasping the rigours of busy, fast-paced university classes, demanding white-collar jobs and exhibition space in Beijing's art venues. Their childhoods may have lasted longer, by Lev Vygotsky standards, had they spent more time on soccer and animal stories. But those children may have more trouble securing prime positions in competitive modern China.

If You Look the Part, You Are the Part

A man selling homes in China more likely than not wears the traditional clothing of his trade: a black coat and short black necktie against a screaming white shirt. A male painter normally sports a goatee and glasses, both culturally accepted hallmarks of artists. A cyclist should wear skin-tight black pants with fluorescent splashes of color. These people might be barely competent as cyclists, artists or sales agents, but the getup gives them a leg up.

People all over China spiff up their personal facades to give the outer world a fixed, positive impression that the individual belongs to a widely recognized group. This emphasis on looking a part starts from the concept of face. It further protects each lookalike from being singled out over any errors and helps ensure a share of any group rewards.

The widely cited concept of face applies to book-and-cover uniformity as the pursuit of a strong public image. The cover lets people pretend to be something they're not, in some cases, heading off ridicule and maybe ruin. During the Cultural Revolution that Mao Zedong sponsored in the late 1960s and early 1970s, for example, most people tried to look drab even if they were actually well-off. In more modern China, many people go all out to show personal progress through their clothes or belongings, so they're seen as maritable and employable.

In one striking example, as described to me by a friend in Beijing, a poor family in China wanted to offer guests a full spread at a traditional Lunar New Year meal and flaunt the guise of wealth. They made a huge steamed fish, a costly meal by most measures, which lasted the whole day. It had to last. It was a slab of wood shaped like a fish.

Face has long been a substitute for law in Chinese societies, I noticed when I came upon University of Massachusetts scholar Jia Wenshan's study 'Facework as a Chinese Conflict-Preventive Mechanism'. Jia says Confucian moral codes — a prescription for how to behave depending on age, status, occupation and family position — have taken the place of Western-style laws for a couple of millennia.

Violations of such vaunted Confucian-coded right and wrong easily meet social disapproval, if for no other reason than they confuse the onlooker, in turn condemning the violators to isolation and maybe lack of resources, Jia argues. Resources might be one's bourgeois wealth, the warmth of a group of friends or access to workplace promotions. Looking too different from others quickly invites this sort of scrutiny — the gateway to disapproval.

Some university students in China still heed the Chinese idiom, "the tallest poppy gets cut down." That means a student who stands up in class too often to answer the teacher's questions will offend the less confident, less competent majority — who can kill the eager over-performer's social life by ignoring him or her for months. The tall poppies, youthful and naïve at the start, had hoped their engagement with teachers would help them learn more and score well on exams. Instead, it deprives them of group membership.

Looking the part helps ensure a share of group rewards. Visibly eager joiners of clubs, classes, volunteer groups and team projects at work probably won't be singled out for underperforming or for trying new things that could threaten old group habits (often lazy ones). They'll all get a cut of any pay, bonuses and public recognition. The head of a ten-person office who strides in one afternoon to announce that everyone will get a bonus for strong monthly profits won't usually be able tell by looking that one or two people did most of the hard work.

In China, companies and other organizations can easily present a false image of competent modernity by spending money for building facelifts. A government department, for example, may be as inept as ever, but it will look a whole different part after brass panelling and black-tinted glass replace old, dirty, white-tiled walls. These facelifts may miss leaky pipes and frayed wires because outsiders can't see those.

With so many offices doing facelifts, to avoid one would look dangerously outlier-ish. Peers and competitors would ask why is so-and-so's building rather ratty when the rest are upgrading? Do they deserve extra funding?

When I worked at the state-run, English-language *China Daily* newspaper, the company remodeled much of its four-story office compound in Beijing. The reception desk moved. The lobby took on the look-feel of a four-star hotel reception zone. Top people's private offices got new wooden floors. Before the remodeling, most of us would edit for grammar, spelling, syntax and political sensitivity rather than adding depth or rewriting stories for readability. Editing stayed that way after the facelifts instead of rising in quality along with the building itself.

In sports, a bike rider like me who wears beach shorts and a T-shirt will be ignored by more professionally dressed cyclists gathered to chat on the roadside, regardless of his muscle mass or the distance he covered to get there. A sweat-absorbent shirt with pockets stuffed with energy bars best convinces other riders that he's ready to take on the next mountain.

Younger Chinese can be seen jumping into the air for photos even though they might normally look glum and calm. The air jump makes them appear dynamic and expressive on WeChat, the way they hope friends will remember them. Anyone who stays grounded with their eyes half-closed for the photo will be scolded as antisocial.

Book-and-cover conformity confirms racial, gender and age stereotypes. For example, older women are, as per convention, supposed to cut their hair short and wear flat shoes. To go with that trend is like telling everyone, "Hey, I'm old." In truth, the individual may prefer other hairstyles and footwear. Perhaps she feels forty.

China, like everywhere, is diverse. Some people scoff at the air-jump group photos. Many don't mind a feast without a fish. Some company heads would rather spend money to train staff rather than redo the walls. Plenty of people see through covers into the real books because they've lived long enough to test people's real abilities or pick up heuristic cues such as the muscle mass on a sloppily dressed cyclist's legs.

Yet the chance to give oneself face and avoid the pain of a tall poppy still motivates numerous people to join groups and look a certain part. If their calculations are right, they will share the group's rewards and avoid any personal criticism, despite sacrificing the chance to shine as individuals.

Obsession with Seeking Achievement

In China, it's common for a comfortably upper middle-class person with no serious health issues, no debt and no deadlines to sidestep play or relaxation. Something always seems to need fixing at home, a blip in the stock market might signal it's time to reshuffle the portfolio and a child's exam score below a ninety demands adult attention. Families such as these let such matters dominate their evenings and holidays. The always-on quest for achievements could start before age ten—to wit: my nine-year-old gallery artist from Chapter 6. Chinese whom I've met abroad, or who just returned to Beijing, express surprise that citizens of the host country define competency in sports and the glow of family bonding as achievements despite zero odds of material payback. In China, family elders might do housework until just before bedtime because they see no value in relaxing in front of a TV, or with a book or even a smartphone. Any leisure reading before bedtime would probably be something materially useful, perhaps a book on how to conquer the capital markets. Some hotel guests even wash their own clothes after a long day of touring to head off a hotel laundry bill.

This relentless pursuit of material achievements reflects a

psychology of accumulation. The psychology has a strong hold due to the historical fear of scarce resources, intense competition for those resources and a side of the multifaceted Chinese 'face' culture that dictates that more of anything material beats its absence.

Lingering on resources and competition, the idea of accumulation suggests that a student who slows studies for play would risk being surpassed by peers in the absorption of knowledge. Knowledge passes tests, and scores lead to university admission. Low or even average entrance exam scores bar most people from admission to big-name Chinese universities. Degrees from the top schools should, the thinking often goes, lead to the ultimate scarce resource: a job that's stable and well-paid.

A family I knew for six years lives in a large, flashy apartment with a giant flat-screen television set, an air-con unit in every room, a recreation centre downstairs and every electronic gadget that a child could dream of. They don't need the money. But the father's parents, who own the flat, require that two of his children study from 7:50 a.m. all day until past the dinner hour so they can excel academically through middle school and get into their city's best high schools—clearly a pipeline to its best universities and later its top jobs. Their existing outsized wealth doesn't give the family enough security to let their kids just run home from school at 4:00 p.m. and watch TV after finishing their homework.

Western psychologists whose work I've read argue children pushed to study at the expense of play turn out to be moderately good in their professions and to enjoy their work less than their peers. I heard one speech by psychology scholar Tal Ben-Shahar who said people who take longish breaks from work have better ideas about how to get their work done—basically the unexpected inspirations one gets in the shower or while taking a walk—because they're away from the minutiae of work but still aware of it.

While a growing number of well-off Chinese urbanites know how to take it easy at the teahouse, the poolside or among the attractions of a foreign country, the Western axiom of "all work and no play make Jack a dull boy" has no widely subscribed Chinese equivalent because it makes little sense against so much competition for resources.

Some people in China get the income they need from family connections. Dad's company might be able to wangle his son or daughter a job, as in a few cases I knew about. But personal income for most depends on achievement alone against competition from tens or hundreds of millions of people with similar ambitions. The ideal Chinese employer's legendary 'iron rice bowl' guarantees of housing, health insurance, a job for life and retirement pay began breaking down around 2000, another reason to chase material gains 24/7, at night and on weekends. Iron rice bowl jobs don't pay much anyway compared to positions in private firms, especially foreign-invested ones. For these reasons, people who are skittish about work income often turn to stocks and property investments to grow their money. Pursuit of this extra income morphs sometimes into steady after-hours work. Children who see their parents working this way stand to absorb the same ethic as adults, even if their day-job income is stable.

The specter of living near poverty with family to support further instills fear followed by the thirst for securing income instead of taking a few breathers. Until the 1980s, just about everyone in China had experienced poverty, directly or through relatives. Even though most Chinese now live above the official poverty line, elders commonly worry about a relapse and younger people tend to learn habits from their elders.

A first-year university student once wrote to my Beijing newspaper Q&A column, saying he worried his chief hobby, a multi-player computer game called 'Half-Life' would "contradict" his studies. He would play 'Half-Life' with roommates and claim some of the highest scores, but the student felt he should maximize study time to get good grades, leading to a high salary from work after graduation, all justifying the tuition paid in full by his parents. "When I was a child, I had the aim of being a businessman, but how can I achieve my ambition if I behave like this?" the student asked me. "The computer games are just like a drug. It's like a snake that charms you and gives you poison if you don't give up immediately." Or was he just less of a dull boy?

Accumulation has obvious face value. A normal human brain, people tend to believe, can hold and apply as much information as it's fed over any period. Lapses in retention are more likely to be seen as a problem with the learner rather than with information overload and a tired brain. Applied to a work setting, this idea of accumulation means the more hours an employee clocks, the more that person get done and the more achievements accumulate.

Many Chinese accept what they see on the surface as a reflection of underlying content, as outlined in Chapter 7. The surface here is a stepladder of palpable, money-related achievements that just keep marching upward. Ideas about how something like a break to play 'Half-Life' might rest the brain, so it can retain more information and better use it, feel wrong from an accumulation perspective. Leisure lacks the face of material progress. It will not make Jack an extra-outstanding boy with more income than his peers.

Mixed-use Mania:
Everything Goes with Anything

Once upon a time in the expatriate quarter of Beijing, I would eat the occasional brunch at a burger and pancake restaurant opened by a Chinese woman who had returned from Canada. She festooned the walls with Western décor. The restaurant opened onto a tree-lined street reminiscent of small-town America. But even before biting into my first hotcake, I knew I was in China. The restaurant would let vendors of pirated music, films and software come inside and peddle table to table. Customers seated by the windows would look out onto the pleading faces of beggars. They would dine to the din of hammers and drills at a remodeling project next door.

Welcome to the mixed use of nearly everything. Most who grow up in China accept odd mixtures of activities sharing a space, even a tight one or one where the quality of an experience depends on a bit of personal breathing room. Those accustomed to this kind of mixed use probably don't mind cars parked on a heavily trodden sidewalk or a hotel lobby pianist's chords clashing with background music issuing from wall-mounted speakers. On one street that I know of, two public schools operate within a hundred meters of multiple nightclubs and a love hotel. The clubs stay open all night until about 7:00 or 8:00 a.m. as children go to school and share a sidewalk with drunks being frogmarched by their friends to a taxi. Some people would feel awkward and empty if outside—say in a heavily zoned Western country—without this cacophony of convergent unrelated activity. Even on corporate websites, images and icons bounce across screens of text to add pizzazz.

These activities are tolerated because so many people grow up living in small spaces with large families, followed for some by stays in university dorm rooms of as many as eight people. Space is basically competitive, and today's crazy get-ahead ethic in China legitimizes occupying spaces that might not be entirely one's own—say peddlers who approach tables in privately operated restaurants—in a country with weak regard for formal rules. Chinese accept a collective approach to just about every angle of life anyway, so mixed use is in sync with the culture. People from other densely populated Asian countries handle hubbub the same way, but China stands out due to its intensity of urbanization, which fosters mixed use.

Arable parts of the country, roughly eleven percent of the total area, were historically packed with people because of a long-standing preference for large families before the one-child policy was instituted in 1978. Most people among the growing population once lacked money to build bigger homes, so they just lived together in tight spaces along with family businesses, farming equipment and livestock. Elders would know poverty from before the 1980s, and for that reason quite a few save objects for future use instead of tossing them to save space.

China became extra-squeezed in the 1950s when Mao Zedong encouraged an explosion of births to power the economy. Chinese leaders after Mao have encouraged people to relocate to already densely populated cities, pushing the urban population past sixty percent of the nation's total before the trend tapered during Covid-19.

As a result of these pressures, Chinese people normally grow up used to being around a lot of people and whatever they're all doing. At the peaks of rush hours, they might stand so sardine-canned on public buses that it's easy to miss stops for lack of a path to the door. On packed trains, it's okay to sit on the backs of seats occupied by other passengers. Buses, cars, bikes and pedestrians often just collect in the streets rather than sticking to particular lanes where they could travel at their natural speeds without the risk of hitting someone else.

I picked up the economics term 'externality' when doing research for this chapter. It refers to the unintended effects, good or bad, of human activity on third parties. Externality is hard to explain in China. Those used to congestion might argue that if mobile street vendors can go table to table in a restaurant without physically interfering with someone else's actual ability to eat—to lift a spoon and swallow—they're not really interfering. A well-adapted person in China should appreciate a scenic landmark next to a construction site by ignoring the site's noise and blight. Externality theory suggests that people can't really ignore the vendor or the construction, as humans are adapted to notice peripheral as well as central cues.

Since the 1980s, the pressure to get ahead economically has increased as the country allows more capitalistic freedom. In that spirit, it's okay to occupy public space for commercial gain. Mobile touts jump into groups of tourists who are busy photographing a monument. I've asked many to back off. Tourist crowds are probably used to commotion, so they don't complain as I did, and any codes for who can peddle where are ignored. It's cool for property developers to occupy public sidewalks with building materials and construction equipment, forcing pedestrians to walk in the road with vehicular traffic.

Some people in China still understand public space such as street surfaces to be up for grabs, not divided by formal legal boundaries. Disregard for formal rules means space is allocated first come first serve. Who-gets-what decisions in China, I've found, depend on the situation and who has the most at stake to influence it.

Sleep-deprived Mariah Zhang once described this push-pull in a letter to my advice column. She was living in a Beijing University dorm room with five other people. Three used computers and were 'still online with the lights on late at night', she griped. "What's worse, they talk and laugh loudly at the same time, which disturbs my sleep." She asked them to stop, but to no avail. The loud people were more numerous and, well, louder. For that reason, they were the first served.

There are those who gripe privately about road menaces and pollution, both the external effects of people's get-ahead ethic. Formal complaints are rare because so many people believe that in China they have no way to change the environment around them.

But before the 2008 Olympics in Beijing, the government made a polluting iron and steel company and a coking-chemical plant leave the capital. The decision said smokestack pollution didn't belong side by side with an international sporting event. Six years later, Chinese then-Premier Li Keqiang declared a 'war on pollution' and was quoted calling smog 'nature's red-light warning against the model of inefficient and blind development'. But day to day, street by street, compound after compound, mixed use remains tightly woven into Chinese society.

The Psychology of Avoiding the Truth

Lies, artful dodges and acts of cheating spark incident after incident in China. For example, a man was once exploding firecrackers outside a row of houses in a small town. It was late, not a traditional holiday calling for pyrotechnics, and the people indoors were trying to sleep. I walked out to ask the man to stop making noise. He denied shooting off firecrackers. As a renter, I've called my property owners about broken appliances. The owners too often say, "That never happened when I was living there." And after discovering a 'tea fee' on a restaurant bill — and protesting that I ordered no tea — the wait crew told me, "We always charge a tea fee. It's our policy." Even if it wasn't.

China, like anywhere, is full of honest people, the giant majority in fact. But the tricks described above are quite common just the same, and they occur so frequently that many Chinese chat for hours among friends about ways to avoid them. Those who try tricks on other people normally have one of two reasons: one, maneuver opportunistically, perhaps in business, around threats and obstacles; two, avoid the harsh fallout of being found guilty of even a common human error. The idea that the victim, not the trickster, bears primary blame for the success of a lie or scam amplifies reason number one. The acute shame piled on people who make common mistakes elevates the second reason. The key is that in Chinese society, people are divided into two groups — insiders and outsiders, strangers and people who are part of one's group. For strangers there may be no sense of responsibility or need to play fair.

Admission of fault, even over a trifle and even among one's own relatives, can bring a sharp rebuke. In times of greater poverty, a gaffe could cause a loss of family income. That loss in turn would spark a panic in acquiring enough food for the family or getting care for a major illness. A child today who spills all to a parent about trouble at school, especially academic failure or problems getting along with teachers, is more likely to be chastised than seated down for a heart-to-heart talk that ends in a friendly smile with nurturing advice. Moms and dads may think this way, at least subconsciously: the same kind of trouble in adulthood would hurt economically valuable relationships with supervisors and clients. Some grown children still contribute to the wider family income in China, because multi-generation households serve as economic networks (see Chapter 13).

Before the 1980s, elders may have had little support outside family if a miscalculation such as planting the wrong crop at the wrong time caught them short of money decades ago. China didn't offer reliable, universal social welfare nets back then. Relief from poverty was entirely a DIY matter. Elders typically pass on to their children a fear that any wealth is fragile and poverty subject to relapse. So, they scold the children about thinking an error-free life is possible. Behind this interaction lurks the notion of shame. A State University of New York study calls shame in China a 'highly painful state resulting in the wish to hide, disappear, or even die'. The study says although it may serve ultimately as a tool toward self-examination on the way to 'perfection', the shame brought on one person extends to family and wider communities — compounding the pain.

If an account manager describes openly how a price quote mix-up led his account to lose money, colleagues may take him less seriously for months or years. They might even see him as a threat to business, though they would quietly learn from his error.

Wrongdoing is associated as well with risk-taking, which, as Chapter 5 explains, is hardly mainstream. That means shame can follow even well-meaning efforts that go awry. The person who books a restaurant to treat visiting relatives knows best. She will be expected to order the food, too. As the meal unfolds, everyone else can freely criticize the fare, the service, the prices and the whole idea of picking that restaurant. (Take it from me: let someone else in your group order. Just try to get the bill.) The critical comments reflect back on the organizer. She set it up; everyone else just went along. Ditto if the co-worker brings on a new client or recommends someone for hire. The new addition had better be good. Whoever starts something risky is expected to accept any fallout.

China still lacks formal criteria, like a well-regarded arbitration system available to all, which would assign shared blame for traffic accidents, contract breaches and building code violations. For that reason, those who accept even a bit of responsibility are often handed it in full, even if the laziness, indifference and forgetfulness of multiple people contributed. In this spirit, a company head in China often singles out an individual to fault for errors that probably involved multiple staffers.

Vast legal grey areas make truth obfuscation even more urgent. Grey areas mean rules exist but they're complex and usually lack enforcement. To succeed in this color zone, companies sometimes pay wages under the table or hire incompetent relatives. What they actually say: those people (grey wage earners) don't really work here, while he (nepotistic hire) actually has a college degree. The companies need a story like that in case law enforcement catches on.

Grey business explains 'tea fees''' on restaurant bills. The operators make extra money from customers who don't protest as I did. Those who complain get the easy lie that everyone is automatically charged the fee. A customer couldn't prove it wrong without surveying everyone else in the restaurant.

Back to the shame factor, dishonest people may know that their victims will feel most of the heat when lies or scams are discovered. Vigilance is the responsibility of the individual rather than the law or society, a function of historically thin legal protections and lack of reliable support beyond the family unit. A tenant who took responsibility for a finger-pointing landlord's broken appliance would feel such deep cutting shame as the 100 percent culprit that he wouldn't think to chase the landlord if he found out later the device was about to break anyway.

Fear of the Ordinary Unknown

Whether or not a severe respiratory disease is spreading through China, fear pulsates through everyday lives. No small number of people travel in groups even to safe, easily reachable places. They don't want to be alone in case something goes wrong. As once the father of a four-year-old in Taipei, I serially ran into extra-cautious mothers who asked whether she was too cold even if she wasn't. She just ran hot and wore long-sleeved shirts on mild days instead of the widely expected four or more layers of clothes for weather of eighteen to twenty degrees Celsius. My daughter would take off layers once outside anyway and generate body heat by moving around. Children may be advised as well to block all sunlight, with window shades or sunglasses, despite its vitamin D benefits. A contingent among the elderly spends a month each year taking steps to avoid ghosts, as recommended by the lunar calendar. Inviting a new friend into one's home in some parts of China is a tense moment, in case the guest sees something inside that reveals unexpected wealth, poverty or some embarrassing private matter.

Fears of negligible risks like these, of course, occur not only in China. I saw it in much of the United States while growing up.

Just about anywhere in the world, I've found, nagging real threats and lack of education about the actual risk-levels, or both, keep a lot of us on edge about our health, safety or reputations. But this state of mind goes deeper in China than in many other countries. Trouble getting scarce resources in the past and modern-day competition in a giant population make China a uniquely tough place where it's worth worrying more than usual.

Lingering for a moment on education, China lacked universal schooling until the 1990s. Lack of formal instruction, naturally, breeds reliance on popular suspicions about elements of the world that can't be proven or disproven. Popular is defined by personal networks. These friends and relatives may be allies, but they're usually not scientists. Suspicions about matters such as health start with a sprig of truth but get distorted without the rigors of testing. Those distortions spread from generation, to generation, to generation. Therefore, drinking cold water in cold weather for as long as anyone can remember in China is blamed for respiratory illness, although no scientists ever said so. My formerly four-year-old child and I drink cold water twelve months out of the year and get sick no more often than the average. Cars last longer if given rests during long trips, some Chinese people also believe.

Now add in the on-again, off-again harsh past of China's past century. People in their sixties and upward usually know about a serious workplace accident or remember the mysterious death of a middle-aged relative. Those disasters preyed on China because, to get by, people would do dangerous subsistence work that wasn't always enough to cover medical care. Younger generations living better now may hear their elders tell these stories and adopt some of their fears as an unquestioned reality.

Then there's the population of 1.4 billion people. Competition for jobs, school admissions and scholarships is hardly known for being fair or transparent, sowing distrust of the huge universe of non-family, non-friend fellow citizens. These misgivings underpin a lot of the fear in China. Formal institutions, including state offices and courts, throughout history have often done their own thing rather than intervening to settle disputes among commoners. That intervention could instill more confidence.

A friend in Beijing who moved to the capital from far-off Yunnan province for school says she's always 'watching her back' in case someone's out to take her money or one of her jobs in the news media, a competitive field. She can't point to any single person or incident. It's just a haunting fear that stems from so much opacity and hyper-competition around her. It seems to her that anyone can snatch a job in Beijing by flattering a superior, treating influential people to a banquet or even sleeping with somebody in power.

Emblematic of the distrust among commoners, villages would once fight one another over land rights. The migratory Hakka people, for instance, battled Cantonese natives in Guangdong Province from 1855 to 1867 as the number of Hakka immigrants grew and challenged Cantonese economic dominance. Governments didn't intervene to parcel out the resources because they saw no glory in it. Passed-down memories of the Hakka-Cantonese conflicts explain why the Hakka may feel more guarded toward strangers today compared to people from other parts of China. In the regions of southern China that Hakkas and Cantonese still call home, friendships take a while to form because of the trust barrier.

Memories of a poor past, modern-day competition and weak enforcement of rules all naturally breed scams. Scams are not uniquely Chinese, but the country is hyper vigilant due to government warnings and mass market films about members of rich families plotting to take money from one another. Rampant telephone and internet fraud rings active since 2000 fan even more suspicion.

I've run across property owners would rather leave a flat vacant than earn rental money lest the tenant destroy their property. My current Hong Kong landlady, as of the writing of this book, thinks I've broken her appliances when I call to report them out of order. The refrigerator makes jackhammer-like noises quite on its own, however. Older people may prefer full-service airlines for their years of proven safety records, shunning newer, cheaper budget carriers that have flown fewer hours. I've been on planes where dozens of passengers switch on their mobile phones a minute after landing, all at once, to text relatives that they've safely arrived. In the past, it was hard to be sure about any vehicle making it, until informed by a passenger that they were all right.

There's one curious loophole: if the source of danger isn't immediately visible, then it's not so scary.

Countless apartment blocks lack structural protection from earthquakes because most occupants have never been affected, so they can't imagine being crushed in their homes when the ground shakes. The idea that small acts such as washing one's hands could prevent spread of disease is literally invisible. On the plus side, face masks are ominously visible. Masks stop infected people from spreading germs and can block the same from getting into one's respiratory system. Masks like no other solution to SARS in 2023 and later Covid-19 appealed to the public because they had the look-feel of an illness barrier. China is something of a show-me society, as described in Chapter 7. That means things are as dangerous as they appear — if they appear. But just about everything else, from the sun to the idea of ghosts, is worth a high level of vigilance.

Eating: Why So Many Things Taste Like Well-Done Chicken

I had the unexpected honor years ago of chatting with Stanley Yen, the elusive, ever-busy former president of the Landis Hotels and Resorts Group in Taiwan. His hotels run restaurants that make pricey tealeaf shrimp and duck soup. Yen spoke more plainly when talking about the origins of his food. Chinese food, whether in China or out in the diaspora, is almost always well done and inundated in heavy sauces because people would once eat that was half rotten, though still not at the disease-carrying stage. And it would taste half rotten if cooked medium-rare without a sauce, Yen explained. The same went for soggy tomatoes and soft, waggly carrots. For those reasons, family chefs would cook everything to the point of super-well-done to rid it of any toxins and soak it in sweet, sour, salty or spicy sauces.

That day on a food-and-beverage media tour, Yen further stabbed at the reasons Chinese cuisine steams with well-done, thinly chopped meats and heavy sauces. It's the same reason exotic animals are popular, and why meat comes from almost a whole animal rather than just a prime cut. It's about frugality, which had obvious appeal to families who lived on incomes that couldn't buy half a hog every day or a fridge to store it. They formed a cuisine around frugality and passed it on and on.

Fast-food chains and supermarkets in China today sell garden salads and burgers cooked medium-rare, and younger consumers eat both for their health. In poorer times, rare meat would be seen as bacteria ridden. Raw vegetables could have been grown in feces and still carry that contamination.

Meat of any kind was once a luxury for the poor, to continue Yen's comment on food. For that reason, households would marinate their main ingredients for preservation. Marinated meat remains common in today's cuisine. And I've eaten in diners around China's subtropical south, where things spoil fast. Chefs there still preserve meats in salt water or vinegar, or through smoke curing and sun drying.

Much of this marinating, curing, drying and use of spices gave rise to the four categories of flavor that define Chinese cuisine. Each one originates from a particular region of China, where the inhabitants developed cuisine according to what the soil and climate there would give back. As I learned from countless chats with Chinese friends, usually in restaurants, each flavor grouping traces to the region of China where it started.

Sichuan Province gets credit for the spicy food that pervades much of southwestern China. Chefs in Sichuan are partial to chili oil, garlic and coriander. Shandong Province in northern China spun off salty sauces for seafood. The rest of the north has kicked in wheat-based foods dumplings and noodles. The lower Yangtze River Delta around Shanghai developed sweet-and-sour sauces, a term familiar to people who eat at Chinese restaurants overseas. Chefs who make Cantonese cuisine, the fourth grouping, treat food with garlic, spring onions, ginger and other pungent spices intended to bring out the meat's underlying flavor.

Aversion to waste, a function of frugal living, reveals a reason that restaurants proudly serve parts of animals that Westerners shun. Chicken feet and duck heads, pig's blood and occasionally a brain appear on menus. Some diners like the flavor; others believe it would be a shame to throw those parts to the dogs if they can nourish a person. The killing of a prized animal merits eating the whole thing, not just the parts that are most succulent and chewable. I find eating an entire animal more environmentally sustainable, to use 2023 lingo, than just carving out boneless chunks and filets as done in the West. (But I've never acquired a taste for the heads and extremities.)

Consumption of non-farm animals started as a way to combat scarcity. Cantonese are known for eating anything with four legs but the table, to quote a joke I hear all over China. A certain calibre of restaurant lures moneyed groups of diners by displaying tanks of live snakes, frogs and gooey monopods from the ocean floor. I stayed in the hotel above one such restaurant when I first arrived China and would gawk in horror until I realised the slithery stuff was selling to some of the neighborhood's wealthiest people. The animals are kept alive to prove the meat is fresh.

A lot of people today prefer the white meat of fish, a chicken leg or a pork sausage. Poorer households couldn't always get those. Some of them learned to catch monopods instead.

Turning to the cabbage, spinach and carrots, a farmer before mechanized agriculture arrived might have grown these with human waste as fertilizer for lack of cleaner but more expensive treatments. The food could still carry bacteria. While checking into this topic, I was naturally tempted to read a culinary anthropology article by the Social Issues Research Centre, a non-profit organization in the United Kingdom. The report says chefs cook food fast, well-done and in small chunks as 'a necessity in China because the use of human excrement as [fertilizer] manure meant that thorough cooking was essential, and the lack of fuel meant it had to be done quickly'.

Today's restaurant menus still reflect the past preoccupations with masking harsh flavors, preserving food or avoiding waste by serving multiple parts of an animal and charging high prices for exotic beasts. Prime examples of smothering organic flavor are the *shui zhu* dishes. 'Shui' means water and 'zhu' is to boil, but that's just a start. These pots mix cooking oil, a bag of dried chili peppers and anise, a spice that numbs the tongue to prepare for a hit of spiciness. That recipe usually attributed to Sichuan Province mutes the original flavour of the fish, beef or chicken. Orders of whole ducks come with beaks, heads and necks. Other parts may be boiled into a duck soup. 'Thousand-year eggs' on the cold-dish menu are a classic preservation case in point. Chefs take fresh eggs laid just days ago and treat them with ash, quicklime, rice hulls and salt for weeks. The process turns the yolk green and the white into brown. The egg won't rot anytime soon.

Lots of Chinese, plus long-term expatriates like me, can't eat enough of these inventions, even today when we can order anything, from anywhere, in the major cities.

Poverty met food in a different way from 1959 to 1961, when millions of Chinese people starved to death due to the failure of harvests. That period known as the Great Chinese Famine arose from drought, poor economic management and untenable changes in agricultural methods. The crisis remains in the memories of older Chinese people. For elders, food might matter so much that their tour groups plan itineraries as much around meals as around sightseeing. Many elders continue to instill in their children a deep respect for food along with a distaste for waste. Chinese banquets generate waste, but largely so hosts can show guests they have ample money to spend and to prove a high degree of hospitality. Waste is less common in private homes. Children even in a lot of wealthy families are taught to keep marinating, preserving and cooking to the max. They would be urged to eat each grain of rice and get every string of meat off the last chicken bone.

Part II
Family and Friends

Family as an Economic and Social Unit

Chinese care passionately about family, I've been told by friends from north to south, from the youth to the aged. I would counter that people of every nationality care about family. It's true, but Chinese can take the concept of family to an extra-high level. There are mothers and fathers who look after their aging parents almost as painstakingly as they care for their own children, who are taught to do the same eventually for their own elders. Three generations can be found living in a single flat, doubling up in bedrooms and even beds when space is cramped. An altar to deceased family members still appears under many roofs and they, the ancestors, reenter the home, in a way, when survivors pray to them.

Family can be a burden and a trap against moving away from home for career achievements, and plenty of millennials will say that as they move to new cities and countries without looking back. They might complain to foreigners like me about how restrictive their parents were or are — controlling friendships, choice of marital partners, college majors and use of income. But most people still see the family as an unbendable economic and social unit because it offers China's most time-tested, reliable insurance policy against just about anything.

In China, a family member is expected to help relatives of any age, sparing little expense. In return, the helper gets helped as needs pop up. A student's mother might take a week's worth of oranges and instant noodles to the dorm room during a study crunch period when there's little time to go shopping. Years later, the student will pool income with her parents to buy a flat. A few larger, wealthier families even buy entire apartment buildings for themselves.

This approach differs from traditional Western families, where eighteen-year-olds are encouraged to leave home, get degrees, find work and establish a new family in a new household. Such an eighteen-year-old is largely left to excel (or not) as a student, worker, spouse and parent, without pressure from parents or extended family.

Historically, the family has always been China's only dependable social unit. Resources were often painfully scarce through dynastic times and into the famines of the early 1960s. Today, despite huge material advances, not-always-fair competition challenges university degree-holders to find coveted career-track jobs—the search for which reached a daunting crunch during in 2022 because of the anti-pandemic controls and other economic setbacks. Even friends can turn into users rather than offering support—an emblem of the crazy ambitiousness that has swept China since the 1980s.

Leaders of China, since records have been kept, offer what my Chinese contacts widely describe as incomplete or unworkable social welfare nets to catch the ill, the unemployed, the elderly or anyone who gets scammed out of their money. Even the best existing welfare programs, though more advanced now than ever, confuse a lot of citizens. Add to it all that the government stopped guaranteeing homes to workers in 1998 and two years later, it mostly quit assigning jobs to college graduates. Youth unemployment was soaring in 2023. Since the 2010s, a Beijing friend complained to me, even families living in homes provided by government bureaus were being asked to go find their own housing.

Going way back in time, lack of social safety nets had pitted common people against each other in competitions so fierce that throngs of villagers have been known to fight physically over land rights. The 1966-1976 Cultural Revolution, in which commoners could expose one another for various alleged crimes and misdemeanors, widened social distrust.

Against this threat outside their front doors, relatives tend to band together. They kick in money, apartments and personal connections, for example, for cousins, nieces and grandparents in need. Connections help the unlucky find work and get out of legal messes. One good friend of mine tried to build a business exporting makeup. She didn't take it hard when sales tapered off. Her father had said he could arrange a job for her in his provincial government office. She also got to live with her family into her late twenties, even though her mom snooped into her e-mails. Room and board were free and it's hard to beat that price.

Bonds remain so strong that some people drop work and scheduled events with friends to help, say, a distant cousin with some minor request such as being escorted to an unfamiliar location. Parents may steer their children away from play dates outside the family so those kids can spend more time interacting with relatives. Just ask my kids. In elementary school, classmates would set up a day in the park or at a shopping mall — sometimes several times — only to have each outing canceled by a parent in the name of a family event.

Views of the outer world as risky and shadowy are reflected in overseas travel. Chinese tourists usually join groups, follow hired guides, stick with Chinese food and charter coaches (more on this point in Chapter 38). These habits extend from the protective family psychology to the race or nation as a bigger family.

Decades of economic progress have made it easier than ever to earn an income in China, but inherited memories of the tougher past can keep families tightly unified. The mother dissuading a child from play dates doesn't think consciously anymore about the Cultural Revolution or a village turf war, but she is probably emulating what her own parents did. The same goes for elders who pay full university tuition for their children and recommend spouses to them after graduation. Older people often hide their health conditions to avoid being a burden, which would distract younger kin from expanding the wider family through marriage and child-rearing.

Directives from elders, backed up by parentally paid university tuition and a parentally supported home for newlyweds, preserve the bonds of family as a self-perpetuating economic unit. While younger people may gripe about the grip of Mom and Dad, they still turn homeward in the end because they almost always get help there. They at least can live and eat for free, perks that make the family roost attractive for young adults at low points, such as job losses and breakups with romantic partners.

The intensity of family ties is chafing a bit now against China's socio-economic modernization, I'd say based on letters I received for my Beijing newspaper Q&A column. Too many over-pampered young adults find it hard to get along with people in complex work settings, once they leave home, the topic of Chapter 15. Some young adults take over family businesses despite boredom with the enterprise, and the resentment grows as they age. Parents are raising pressure on their adult children in with new fervor, my column letters indicate, because older teens have more non-family options than ever, from moving abroad to joining heavy metal bands. WeChat brings friends into the family living room via phone, and they chip away at parental influence at home.

China's new wealth has put a curious stress on well-off families, too. The mutual aid that underpins relationships can suddenly become superfluous, challenging an aid giver's sense of utility and duty. A second-year university student in Hubei Province once wrote to my column that he felt guilty when he couldn't help his parents economically on their farm—because they didn't need any extra support. "They have been working very hard all these years to pay for my expensive tuition," the letter says. "I appreciate their painstaking efforts, so I studied hard at school and planned to show my filial obligation to them. My plan for summer was to help them with farm work. However, both my parents objected and just prodded me into studying."

In knottier cases of surplus wealth, relatives hand one another money for the stock market and business startups. They often make no formal plan for paying anyone back. When an investment of this sort fails, guilt or hatred bubble up inside the two parties. Backstabbing surges. But ultimately these debtors and creditors continue to answer the call of the higher order of family as an unbreakable social and economic unit.

Chinese-Foreign Marriages: Is There a Natural Attraction?

It's hardly the most elegant phrase, but here it is anyway: yellow fever. This mosquito-borne disease common in the tropics colloquially describes people from non-Asian countries who are attracted to Asians. In the big cities such as Beijing and Shanghai, men of European descent turn up in restaurants, malls and subway cars with Chinese girlfriends and wives. Sometimes, too, a Chinese man is spotted out with his girlfriend or wife of European descent. Some 'language exchange' ads are aimed more at dating than swapping Chinese lessons for English. Clearly a lot of Chinese and foreigners like each other romantically.

They pair up at first because each side sees the other in a shining light. But relationships that work out over a few years to a lifetime take some cross-cultural heavy lifting. The following sequence of Sino-foreign hookups merges the stories of multiple friends and my own, though sparing names and other details to protect us fever patients and our partners. And I've agonized over the pronouns here. Chinese men and foreign women do date and marry, in my observation, but significantly less often than Chinese women and foreign men get tied up. I normally use 'he' in this chapter to represent foreign guys and 'she' to describe Chinese women.

Western men may be captivated initially by Chinese women's looks: he's thinking they seldom get fat compared to peers in other countries, especially outside Asia. They often wear dresses and tight pants instead of unisex clothes. Hair trends long. Some foreign men are drawn as well to Chinese women's conservative outlook on relationships. For example, a woman might not mind raising a family and looking after the household instead of pursuing a career, freeing the man to work as hard as he wants outside the home. In Western countries, men and women are supposed to be all but equally drawn into high-stakes careers. Both may be expected to take care of children.

Chinese women may hold a stereotype that Western men are either rich or have easy access to wealth because they come from countries that are historically wealthier than China. That stereotype triggers the woman's practical side, which says dating should lead quickly to marriage with wealth not far behind. If he's rich already, she expects to share his wealth. If he's not rich yet, she might figure marriage will generate a passport that lets her live in his rich native country. There, she can start accumulating money. (A lot of Chinese nationals don't realize daily expenses might run higher in a lot of Western countries compared to China. I've stunned friends by walking them through an imaginary middle-class budget in San Francisco Bay Area where I lived many of my adult years.) Women in China are known, too, for pursuing older men from their own country due to the allure of their money. Those men could be bosses or teachers.

A few Chinese people prefer foreigners as well for the stereotype that we cherish the magic of romantic dates rather than pushing for marriage after a series of dinners and carefully planned outings, as is common in China.

Every person's outlook differs a bit, of course, and the marriage-money link is not unique to China. China is also much better off now than a few decades ago, but a collective memory of poverty lives on, so the idea of getting rich fast without a lifetime of hard work can still appeal to even solidly middle-class people. A woman's parents might push the get-rich marriage scheme even more than she herself does, because as older people they had trouble with money in their earlier years. Like peers in other Asian countries, women in China typically look down on blue-collar jobs as unhealthful, poorly paid and low status. To marry into wealth implies a certain cleverness, which adds status.

Within months, the woman could figure out she's just a trophy wife and walk out. The man could wish after a while she'd get a job and resent signs that he's being used for his money.

Yet cross-racial couples in China can also last long and successfully. They might have two proud careers and at least as many children. To get there, one and probably both sides probably has become accommodated to the other in ways that were not natural at first. Most couples who outlast an introductory period are not working off looks or money. They arduously strive to bridge divergent cultural expectations.

Here are some common hotspots that couples need to extinguish:

Chinese partners tend to want marriage within a couple of years of dating rather than a longer phase where they share an apartment while unwed and see what develops. A woman who wrote to my Beijing newspaper Q&A column said it best about a French boyfriend. It was fun at first: "He is kind, humorous and rational while I am just like a dreaming girl. I rushed to say 'I love you' in French but he is… very cautious to say I love you. He needs more time for acquaintance." Then he left her.

They probably expect their parents to get heavily involved, too, from co-organizing a wedding to living in the same household and calling the shots on childcare. (See Chapter 15 for more details on the parental impact on marriage.) Lots of foreigners aren't used to those setups, so they might recoil at first. However, over time foreigners in the better marriages realize the spouse's parents usually contribute heavily to the household, if they live together, as well as to the extended family income. Those contributions cut to the Chinese view of family as an enduring economic and social contract, as outlined in Chapter 13.

Western men may feel irritated if their Chinese spouses keep quiet in social gatherings. The partner probably does that because she was admonished as a kid to avoid any embarrassing mistakes and later because she realized saying too much gave strangers fodder for gossip. If the foreigner didn't grow up that way, he will find it rude that his wife won't make more than a line or two of friendly chatter with friends and colleagues. Chinese women chafe if a man too often brags, even in the spirit of beer-and-football conversation where guys just say whatever they want for a laugh. A man who hogs space in casual chatter could offend the woman's sense of social order in a group of equals.

And, she might wonder, what's up with the bike in the living room and the cabinet full of board games? I get into this with my wife. Then there's my five-storey bookcase. Westerners like me tend to pursue sports, games and literature, just for fun rather than to gain such knowledge to get a job promotion. These pastimes cost time and money, so a Chinese partner may question whether anything so impractical is worth the capital. Most Chinese have dabbled in serious hobbies over just the past twenty years, because only over these two decades has China grown prosperous enough to let its citizens consider spending time on something that doesn't pay materially. Foreign men in turn may resent a wife's pressure to spend an uncomfortable share of their joint earnings for practical gain even when everything seems to be in place. She will normally want to buy at least one piece of property and put the children in top local schools, including private ones, from kindergarten upward. If the family still lives in China, she hopes the child will graduate from a key elementary school onward to her city's best middle school and then to a top university. She's trying to get ahead in a world she still considers dicey and competitive, even if the family already lives well with no palpable danger of falling behind.

Long-term relationships are not fever. Each side usually has a natural ability to empathize across cultures and make compromises.

Who to Impress if Marrying a Chinese Person

Hardly anyone out there can say their parents don't somehow influence a marriage. But in China, the role of Mom and Dad, especially Mom, is especially crushing. Parents generally expect to at least help pick the mates of their young adult children. Women should prepare to live with their in-laws, though not all will end up there. Newlyweds should set aside money for their spouses' aging parents. Every family operates differently, and there's a progressive backlash that doesn't believe in any of these traditions and plenty of 20-somethings resent parental pressure before or after marriage, but the average couple in China still builds much of their lives around parental expectations.

Chinese people in the more conventional category see marriage as an extension of the larger family network, which as outlined in Chapter 13, works as a social and economic support system. For that reason, parents in these families take a strong role. They want their children to marry people who can capably contribute to family and may spend years nagging their young adult progeny to get on with it. Elders in the network often believe they have extra responsibility in choosing new members, so serious boyfriends and girlfriends should prepare to impress the other person's mother. Foreign spouses are no exception.

Here are key things successful spouses-to-be know and the steps they take. I've compiled this advice from chats with friends in Beijing—including with young people's parents—letters to my newspaper Q&A column and my own many missteps. The tips here are boilerplate, however, not rules; actual courses of events may vary.

In their early dating phase, the love-crossed avoid the other side's parents. There would not be an informal occasion such as an American teenager bringing his new girlfriend over for an energy drink after school. Chinese parents who encounter a same-age, different-gender friend of their own offspring first presume the two are thinking about marriage. Dating has only that practical purpose, conservative elders tend to believe. Mothers and fathers hope to see their children find a mate before age thirty, which is ideal for bearing kids and adding to family income sooner rather than later. For this reason, young Chinese seldom mention girlfriends or boyfriends to their own parents until they're pretty serious about marriage. My wife put off making a parental introduction in the first few months when we were dating, which we did for more than a decade.

Before marriage, partners should discuss what to expect from elders. For example, do any in-laws anticipate living with the new married couple and eventually receiving home care? China has a shortage of safe, affordable, compassionate retirement homes, leaving care to younger relatives. Do anyone's parents worry too much about everything the adult child does, from brands of clothes worn to elective courses picked at the university? That micromanagement would show over-protectiveness founded on fear. The fear is that in opaque China, trouble could befall a child without oversight. Struggles today to carve out a middle-class living in China's cutthroat rush for riches make mothers and fathers all the more protective of adult children. Parents of this mindset want the child to have a life of prosperity without struggle. If all this fawning has spoiled the young adult, he or she might enjoy the attention and expect a spouse to care about him the same way.

Millennials should ask their romantic partners about how their parents were moulded psychologically by the Cultural Revolution, a decade from 1966 when common people hid assets to avoid being publicly humiliated by Red Guards. If they had a hard go of it, Mom and Dad might feel extra suspicious when meeting new people. The famine of the early 1960s, another landmark period in China's 20th Century socio-economic journey, often left a sense of urgency about breadwinning for the family, meaning pressure on any working-age spouse to earn and share a steady income.

When eventually meeting the parents, the newcomer usually takes large sparkly gifts that convey respect and reflect the ability to spend real money. A dozen polished pieces of imported fresh fruit wrapped in colored paper and arranged in a basket will do perfectly. Conversation normally starts safe, from weather and traffic to an outline of what everyone does for work. A generosity showdown often follows: in-laws treat the would-be spouse to a dinner, challenging the guest to pay for dessert. If the father offers to pay for a cab to take the guest home, the guest should put the money back in his pocket. I used to lose these contests with the in-laws until I learned to devise in advance ways of handing back money or out-gifting the other side. Sometimes the process was immediate, other times, it could go on for months or years. These acts cast the partner as a provider rather than a taker.

During later encounters with parents, marriage hopefuls

should play up palpable achievements such as academic degrees and stock market wins. Those laurels make a marriage partner look like a capable, responsible caretaker. My mother in-law was wowed, though unbeknown to me, when I drove to the family house in a new, albeit cheap car, because she knew I had bought it with my wages four years out of college rather than with help from my family.

Some mothers and fathers still spouse-shop for their adult children, an extension of arranged marriages that were more common before the 1950s. Children technically make the choice nowadays, but parents lobby hard against people they fear will be too lazy or irresponsible to provide income. Mom and Dad in these cases have probably instilled in their children a sense of loyalty to home, the socio-economic network, for so many years that their opinion on marriage has huge impact. I met a mother's wrath once for just being a normal friend of her daughter. Her fear of possible dating had her calling and texting her to quit hanging out with me.

If a wedding is allowed to proceed, parents usually want a blow-out ceremony. In a lot of cases, newlyweds themselves pay the full bill and don't go cheap. Usually whatever amount the wedding guests give in red-envelope gift money offsets costs. As the wine bottles and plates empty of boiled shrimp pile up, genuinely excited in-laws fete the couple. Many will urge the bridegroom to drink and sing. One uniquely and still common Chinese spectacle forces the bride to pass a raw egg up one leg and down the other through the groom's still-fastened trousers, for all to see. Every moment, especially the inevitable gaffes, will be photographed and talked about for decades.

At some time during that ceremony, the baby question starts to circulate. Babies go a long way in pleasing traditional in-laws, so the question should be when rather than if. I've never forgotten advertising agency head Tom Doctoroff's suggestion in his book *Billions: Selling to the New Chinese Consumer*. He argues that, per traditional ways of thinking, women without children had no practical use. That's especially true of families who rely on their overall headcounts for income. A grown baby adds earning potential. "Wives' most sacred duty was to bear children and fiercely protect them until they reached maturity and could contribute to the clan's well-being," Doctoroff writes of China's not-so-distant past.

In the years to follow, if a married couple doesn't live with either partner's parents, weekend socializing should involve in-laws, as should vacations. As their incomes grow, both spouses normally pool money to help either side's elders who are sick or need a new apartment. Elders give back everything they can, but if they're low income, they won't be able to kick in as much as their adult children. A married couple at this point takes the lead in ensuring prosperity for the extended family, rewarding the in-laws' careful selection of a responsible spouse.

Shyness Around Strangers if Scolded, or Coddled as Children

Pervasive silences in Chinese boardrooms, classrooms and even festive ballrooms perplex many a newcomer to China – and a more talkative foreigner like myself tossed into the mix might instinctively respond by filling the quiet spaces with chatter. Chinese may describe themselves as 'shy' to explain ominously long, awkward silences at these events. But some people simply don't want to speak. They feel safest looking at everyone else from behind a glass of water. They would sense no social disapproval, nor would they imagine they're missing out. And in a lot of ways they're right.

As letters to my newspaper Q&A column told it, people who were scolded or over-protected as children veered toward the quiet side. Those scolded for goofs at home, per this theory, would fear a backlash from saying anything that listeners in a tense, crowded or public setting would consider imperfect. The coddled might figure, why bother at all with talking to strangers? There's no need to take that risk when family fills my social needs.

No small number of children are routinely scolded, even

punished, by Mom and Dad when they miss their ideal grades at school, for instance a final exam score under ninety-five. My own children have told me these stories about their classmates. The classmate could be admonished as well to win at sports rather than just enjoy the team spirit and good vibes that one's body exudes after a workout. The scolding type of parents will often do a humbling autopsy if a child finishes below third place in an individual sport. Before a public appearance, say a school-sponsored reading contest, these children probably rehearse under the scrutiny of parents who are expecting a win. My kids had trouble competing with them without the same windup. Victory for the other parents could be a high score. It could be a prize. It could be the teacher's verbal approval. To advance that cause, some parents even write their children's lines for them to memorize before speech contests.

Another scenario: children are not pressured at home. They make a few mistakes on stage and don't win every event. But they speak with confidence that helps them year after year in getting used to an audience. China is rife with these young adults, meaning plenty of parents believe in letting their children, and fate, take their natural course.

Yet 'shy' remains the usual buzzword. By high school, most students follow or at least grasp this dominant ethic, the one passed on by classmates from families that are quick to criticize: be great or be chastised. There are classmates who whisper to one another when a fellow student slips up during a presentation. The gaffe is more likely than any underlying achievement—as in, "Hey, I had fun anyway"—to spark chatter over the next couple of days. Peers would feel relief that it wasn't *they* who goofed. Those who gossip about little goofs do more harm than just causing flashes of humiliation. In extreme cases, they discredit the victim in front of so many peers and teachers that basically no one expects the mistake-maker ever to perform well.

"I am a freshman at Anhui University," a classic case-in-point named Mao Dejun wrote to my Q&A column to complain about his own silences. "I am not a boy with too much shyness. I can make conversation easily. But when I go to the blackboard to give a talk, facing all the students in the class, I always get nervous and cannot speak well, even if I have prepared well before class."

Parents and well-meaning teachers who pressure students to avoid mistakes may be thinking that in the population so huge, resources are scarce and only the top people can take the best jobs out there. Those who falter too often would struggle more economically, raising the fear of slipping back into poverty that was widespread before the 1980s. Children, these elders believe, should master perfection early in life.

Once into adulthood, children raised under these pressures typically strive to speak perfectly around teachers, employers and other providers of rewards. The perfect don't mind chatting up a stranger. They have nothing to fear. But many more will tiptoe through meet-and-greet events. When not-so-chatty people are sent to a professional conference, they talk enough to scoot by without raising questions. It's socially awkward to miss an office party. Those fearful of speaking might speak at these occasions only when asked questions.

Coddled children have a different calculus, I've found. If they can share their full colors with a warm, welcoming family, there's no need to risk a possibly derisive, not-so-welcoming reaction from people outside home. The over-protectiveness probably starts with the many mothers and fathers who distrust strangers. Their distrust stems from decades of reasons: resources are scarce but people are not, laws are weak and governments from century to century have paid little attention to the affairs of ordinary people. Strangers can get ahead in this environment by exploiting information gathered from casual chatter. Someone's wayward comment about looking for a new job could prompt a colleague to tell that person's current boss, an obvious embarrassment, and start pushing to take over the job seeker's current position. But then, what if the job search fails?

Oodles of strangers in China do listen compassionately and help instead of hurt. I met more than my share of them. It's just hard to know for sure who won't hurt.

Some parents warn their children directly about these risks. Others hint at dangers by urging the child, of any age, to spend as much time as possible at home and discourage get-togethers with friends. The same mother and father would see the child — especially an only child — as a treasure who needs to be protected. These parents are most likely to intervene in problematic friendships, decide whom the child will marry and step in to sort out academic setbacks. In times good or bad, this kind of child is always the center of protective attention. Adults who were over-parented because the outside world was considered risky naturally look toward family for companionship.

Whether scolded or coddled, young adults may be in for some awkward moments when faced with more outgoing people, including foreigners who are more comfortable with strangers. These gregarious partygoers will ask shy strangers in the mix a few easy personal questions as openers to a chat where both sides share themselves. They might wait several soda sips for replies. When none emerges, more extroverted people might just talk away about themselves for minutes on end as if narrating a resume into a microphone. This one-sided chatter can actually relieve a more inhibited counterpart, who will smile and find it entertaining. By doing most of the talking, the stranger shows no sign of being a harsh critic or a devious misuser of any information shared in conversation.

Children Without Siblings Struggle to Find Friends

Sharing doesn't always come naturally in China. At work, a colleague might say only hi, bye and other compulsory one-liners instead of chatting. A business partner may be garrulous when making deals but not know what to say during a long wait in the railway station before flying to the next client visit. I've met these people — well-meaning, normal people. They get their work done and do their share in business. They've learned basic compatibility skills, just not a lot of social experience.

No small number of these people grew up without siblings, by law. The One-Child Policy initiated in 1978 saw to that, until it began easing in earnest from 2016. By then, the effort to control population size had clearly created socio-economic problems, such as a shortage of workers and burdens on single couples to care for two sets of parents plus their own child. The lack of brothers and sisters under-equips a lot of only-children to share, chat, negotiate and gauge the likely reactions of same-age people around them. Brothers and sisters are effective at teaching that skillset. Only-children might struggle to form deep adult friendships as a result.

I grew up with a brother and not in China, so I was a newcomer, times two, to this phenomenon and looked to the academics for guidance. Single-child families 'produce self-centred little emperors and empresses", according to a Harvard Asia Pacific Review article. It says single children lean toward 'self-seeking instincts' and rely more on their parents in adulthood compared with youngsters who grew up with siblings. Quite possibly, they were showered at home with attention and fancy possessions during childhood, I imagined. China became relatively prosperous during the one-child years, so only-children received more luxuries and opportunities (chances to attend universities, for example) compared with people raised before the one-child policy took effect.

And such luxury-like treatment at home makes the world outside feel harsher by comparison. Back to the academics, I found a paper by three Australian universities called 'Little Emperors and the 4:2:1 Generation'. It says China's only-children are less trusting, less competitive and more pessimistic compared to peers in previous generations.

Only sons and only daughters realize something's wrong when they reach college, if not sooner. The campus surrounds them with thousands of people their same age from only-child homes. They want to fit in and build friendships. Some of these eighteen-year-olds lean on Mom and Dad for social support but find that hard over large geographic distances, so relations with classmates take on crucial weight.

Problems may blossom when students find the lack of brothers or sisters has left them without the habit or ability to carry on a conversation, a trait that's obviously useful in friendships. Conversant people would start off with small talk, listen reflectively, use neutral, non-defensive body language and pick topics of mutual interest. Their sibling-less peers grow nervous instead in front of the other party. It's easier to chat with fellow students during class because of the formal structure and discussion topics assigned by teachers. Once out of class, the socially under-equipped are on their own with no guidelines. A potential conversation companion is free to stay or go.

Not everyone sweats over getting the match lit to make friends. Those who fancy themselves as emperors or empresses surrounded by commoners don't even care to fret over an opening line. (See Chapter 16 for details.)

Getting nervous is just one social barricade owing to lack of experience. A first-year student at a university near Shanghai once wrote my Beijing newspaper's Q&A column that a roommate in her dormitory was from the countryside and "quite curious about everything I do and everything I have. Everywhere I go, she will ask me where I want to go, and each time I come back, she will ask me where I have gone. She also asks me a lot about my [other] roommates. The girl even asks about my parents' jobs and things like that. I am quite an independent girl and don't want to be disturbed like that. But she's my classmate, and we are together almost the whole day. Thinking of this as the beginning of my four-year college life, I feel really at a loss."

The letter writer's first instinct is to snub this roommate rather than share her life. If the letter writer grew up without siblings, all but certain, given her age at the time, she would easily recoil at her roommate's overtures because she's not used to constant, intimate conversation with someone outside the family. Urban dwellers sometimes look down anyway on people from the countryside. The inquisitive roommate perhaps finds the letter writer snobbish by resisting her curiosity. In her defense, families in farming areas often operate like micro-villages where everyone keeps up with everyone else's affairs in case things go wrong. The roommate's aunts, uncles and cousins might have lived within a few minutes' walk. She would have grown up around lots of people, not just her parents, a credit to her social skills.

By the time people like these letter writers reach their first jobs, they will have learned through trial and error with classmates the basics of getting along without family. A lot will still struggle with friendships, however, and continue looking to Mom and Dad for their core social support.

In marriages, an only-child might still feel more allegiance to parents than to a spouse after so many years of unconditional support growing up. Either spouse may expect the other to offer unbridled attention, such as the kind he or she received as children. I ran across a report by the former China.org news outlet describing only-child spouses as 'not used to restraining themselves and taking care of and showing consideration and respect for others'. As a result, China.org said, "There will be more friction between husband and wife, and none of them would like to compromise."

In 2016, China ended the one-child policy that it had implemented to control a surging population at a time of economic distress. The government started letting couples raise two children to foster a large national workforce and help ensure couples have faithful caretakers — their own grown children — after retirement. And in 2021 the government raised the maximum to three children per couple — though many city dwellers couldn't afford three, maybe not even two. These larger families will inevitably spawn a generation of children who learn from siblings to share and communicate, leaving them with skills to form fast friendships as adults.

No Favor Ever Forgotten — no Debt Either

The favor bank is the world's oldest lender as well as the most popular one in China. Newcomers to the country like me need not wait long before we get asked for free foreign-language lessons, help contacting an embassy or seed investment for a tiny startup. Some of the people who ask are mere fleeting acquaintances. Chinese regularly ask one another for small loans and job connections. Requests can be abrupt, without much feeling around for whether the person being asked is really willing. Just about everyone benefits because most people pay back these favors by offering their own free services. A friend or even that casual acquaintance seeking a favor today expects to be asked for one back later.

These exchanges are hardly unique to China but occur there with particular frequency because of a historic lack of reliable, formal and affordable channels to get ahead in life.

Many Chinese turn to private networks for almost anything that's costly, competitive or hard to find. That's why friends would ask me if I could introduce them to visa officers in the US Embassy. I'm American and they figured I could smooth their visa applications, present or future. The embassy doesn't work that way, but it was my friends' thoughts that counted. China lacks surefire social security of the type that would rescue every down-and-out farmer and unemployed construction worker. Successive governments have busied themselves with matters of state, leaving commoners to make it largely on their own. Some dynasties encouraged neighborhoods to take care of their own less fortunate, and associations would form around people with a common surname, meaning they once belonged to the same family and should take care of one another.

Working people might expect the biggest benefit to come from daily wages, but pay for many remains low, especially when held up to cost-of-living surges in Beijing and Shanghai. Well-paying jobs are hard to find in a population about 1.4 billion.

Only in this century did banking become a reliable source of savings and loans for the public. Before that, people lent money to those whom they trusted. Many modern Chinese still turn first to friends and family because they don't trust the banking system 100 percent. I recall the anxious, well-dressed Chinese woman who walked into my Beijing news bureau years ago to tell us that employees of a local bank branch had stolen money from her account. She proved it with paperwork, and we wrote the story.

For these reasons, common people normally expect to survive on their own. If they don't have enough of their own resources, they can turn to friends and family for help because they're already close-knit. Adult children not uncommonly live at home to save money, for example. Two or three generations might even pool money for major expenses, such as one person's medical bills.

Favors aren't necessarily repaid act by act. Someone helped today might not seek a favor for months or years. Many Chinese help their wealthy and powerful friends as an insurance policy. Someday they may need that loan, seed capital or job, though it's not always clear when, if ever.

We foreigners in China meet people who are eager to offer free tour guide service. A local might buy a foreigner lunch with no quid quo pro. One day if suddenly in need of translation, editing, language training or advice on applying to graduate school in the foreigner's homeland, that person would feel empowered to ask. I had more than one friendship of this type while working with the Chinese staff at *China Daily* in Beijing. Western teachers in China know this give-and-take especially well. Students see those teachers as valuable reserves of foreign language instruction, letters of recommendation and tips on getting into graduate schools. Better teachers call it their professional duty to help anyway and perhaps never ask students for help in return. But they could ask. The student would help back. I confess to asking a few former students in Beijing to help me find news sources because my just phoning strangers up for comment in China yielded pathetically little.

Favor-banking carries on largely because it's so habitual now. And while modern Chinese can hire professionals to translate, consultants to prepare applications for foreign universities and banks to lend money, those services all charge fees.

Debt-favor exchanges do occasionally get messy. Families who have little money at first might not mind borrowing money from relatives who are just slightly better off, for example. But if the lender suddenly needs that money back but can't get it right away, it's awkward because the debtor is a relative, part of an exclusive and unwavering economic unit as outlined in Chapter 13. The creditor probably tries in this case to borrow that sum through yet another personal connection.

More mess follows when a creditor feels some deed has

a vast, unquantifiable value that should be repaid over a long period. Chinese immigrants whom I've known in the United States may stay up at night, after working ten-hour restaurant shifts, to help relatives in China apply for their own US green cards. Those immigrants might offer the newly arrived sibling or aunt a place to stay for a few months, even in a house with little space. Days later, the veteran US denizen helps the newcomer adults find jobs and their children enroll in local schools, both processes that can be daunting for a recent immigrant. Eventually the newcomers will figure out how America works and make money. The original benefactor could expect their beneficiaries at that point to treat them to an unspecified number of family banquets. They won't say anything to each other but both sides acutely sense the weight of the expectation. However, genuinely generous benefactors expect little in return, though they would appreciate the odd show of gratitude.

Daily interaction between the Westernized children of these debtors and creditors even takes a hit. The newcomer's sons and daughters, once in their twenties, tend to figure out the source of tension and feel inferior to their cousins from the family that did all the upstream hard work. Not from China, they might resent the whole favor-debt cycle and wonder why it exists. No wonder Chinese millennials don't mind borrowing from real banks and outsourcing other business, despite the costs. These formal channels are reliable, affordable and clean.

What the Elderly Look Forward to Most

After retirement, traditional older people in China seldom plan rugged overseas adventure trips or go live alone along a scenic coastline to write the great Chinese novel. Life for them has already been an adventure. A rugged trip could spell injury. A novel might not make money. Seclusion is lonely. Of course, a growing number of older people are shifting that trend. I've seen them on mountainous hikes and in iffy business ventures. But they're still a minority.

China's elderly normally want to enjoy their lives in cautious comfort, at last, in the ways that recent Chinese history has denied them. They would want instead a run of years that are free of financial risk, illness and fractured families, replaced instead by modest luxuries and everything as close as possible to their grown children. No one knows better than the elderly that life is full of risks and surprises, and more than 297 million Chinese are older than sixty. Because of nationwide trends in the decades when they grew up, they've almost all experienced some level of poverty, a measure of socio-political chaos and questions about how much to trust other people.

Aversion to risk comes naturally for someone who spends decades not sure whether one's savings can cover daily expenses or how they'll be affected by political chaos. A wish for modern comforts arises from chronic lack of them in the past. And now most people can move up because of steady gains in average personal wealth across China. Living near children, in the same town, if not the same flat, represents closeness to the most trusted people ever. Solitary retirement could leave someone helpless in an emergency. Older people, in China like anywhere else, probably hope someone will be around to hear stories from the past and share what may be the best years of their lives. A foreigner such as myself who meets people in their seventies and older will get to listen to these stories after a brief phase of establishing trust and a common spoken language.

Plunging into business reeks of the risk of losing money, which would smell like a new onset of poverty. Retirement in a foreign country, even if cheap and scenic, is full of X factors, rather than the smooth post-hardship life so many people hope for. Retirees from Western countries might relish adventures because they lived through decades of stable income under systems that protect their gains. Their Chinese peers didn't.

Risk-free retirement ideally starts in the city where the elder has lived longest and knows people. It means forming, if not continuing, a gentle but consistent exercise routine. Speed walking, calisthenics and swimming are top draws, as I observed for years in Beijing. The idea is to live past eighty, which is considered a successful age in China from a health standpoint. I had a friend whose grandmother died at eighty and he was as happy as he was sad because she had survived eight decades. I had a colleague who kept his mind sharp reading, practising the art of hand-brewing tea, studying English and part-time copy editing. He was in his late sixties 60s at the time and eager to share his mind-sharpening tools with me as a foreigner willing to sit and listen to him chat.

A lot of retirees gather in public parks for Chinese chess and cheerful chatter with friends, who meet up just by passing by the same bench around the same time every day. Central Beijing's Ditan Park and Ritan Park are classic examples.

Later in a typical risk-free retirement day, one might go home and read a book or take up, say, Chinese calligraphy. Luxury levels for the aging depend on personal wealth. Some retirees pool money with family members, their grown children for example, to buy an apartment and remodel it. Retirees with spare cash do visit places they have heard about over the decades — but travel primarily through the safety of group tours: Mt Emei in China; outside, the beaches of Thailand or the shopping malls of Hong Kong. Group tour operators usually sort out the transportation, hire guides and arrange Chinese-language interpreters.

Living near family is typically a top goal for smooth retirement. Chinese prized family unity long before the modern era. Because of these bonds, elders often expect grown children to care for them when they are sick or out of money. They probably hinted around about that when the children were still pre-teen. We work hard now to earn money and provide a home, parents might say, and how nice if our most trusted kin could care for us when we get old. My friends in their twenties through fifties report their parents use half-cryptic pseudo-questions such as, "What am I going to do if I get really sick someday? I think I have enough money but, oh, what if...?" And my friends are supposed to come back with, "Don't worry, Mom, I'll handle that when the time comes."

Grown children may are likely to ask first that their moms and dads help care for grandchildren. Grandparents usually welcome that task because they're in a low-stress phase of life. Less stress means more patience to help raise children without the rigors of shaping them into competitive adults with great personal habits and a thirst for study as a parent would. The parents are freed up to work, which they might otherwise sacrifice to look after children who get off school before China's standard 5:30 p.m. quitting time.

Living near grown children gives older people a chance to rekindle family warmth. Middle-aged adults in the past often had to figure out how to get by for spells with little income, even to the point of splitting their young family: Mom or Dad would work in another city while the other stayed home with any kids. Old age might give people their first chance to enjoy time with children and grandchildren.

Strangers Are Competitors in Disguise

Competition is brazenly obvious in China. I noticed while stuck on traffic jam-mired buses in Beijing that cars and pedestrians around us all but physically push to get into fast-closing empty spaces on the street. The contrast would be a twenty-second sacrificial pause here and there to accommodate someone slower — notably a car slowing for a guy on foot. Farmers in some parts of China have tilled the land so much that it has few nutrients left, making it virtually unusable for future generations without fertilizers and other inputs. Their predecessors needed food and lacked the luxury of thinking ahead even for their own offspring who would inherit that land. Sports teams struggle sometimes because players vie with one another for individual achievement rather than pooling their strengths collectively behind the group.

The masses — the thousands of souls who anyone meets in a given day — are still largely seen as competitors who are engaged in cutthroat rivalry for resources no matter how fleeting or meagre those may be. Such get-ahead antics in public spark frequent complaints among Chinese that the country lacks a strong civil society. Key reasons: resources really are scarce, despite China's accumulation of wealth since the 1980s, and the organizations that would help support a civil society remain weaker than their counterparts in other countries.

In a model civil society, people help strangers on the premise the favor will be returned, though perhaps later, randomly and by a third person. Chinese have deep helping instincts like anyone else and express them liberally in non-competitive situations such as among friends. But among strangers, they tend to feel a crush to get ahead and even fear every move could catapult the strangers toward first place or knock them back.

Just a small percentage of China's population is poor by government measures today, but centuries of poverty and scarcity of goods as elemental as food have hardened much of the population into resolute go-getters. The fear of losing access to resources lurks especially among many of China's elderly who had struggled to make enough money to support their families. Today younger people—cautioned by elders about historical scarcity even if their family is living well now—vie for high-paid jobs and just about everyone in the cities jousts for positions in traffic, on subways, for kindergarten slots and in lines for a range of services in a country where overpopulation amplifies the scarcity of resources.

Children growing up now might see Mom and Dad cutting in lines to save time. Those children at later ages will be tempted to imitate what they saw because it formed such a strong early-life impression. Young teens may be urged at home to pursue university degrees that generate well-paid jobs and to marry people with access to money. Any wealth generated is expected to be shared with the whole family, as outlined in Chapter 13. Elders often encourage their children just out of college to spend time with classmates who have employment connections. University students commonly regret leaving the 'innocent' years of study to start competing with their own classmates for jobs, as I heard from my own students in Beijing, plus letter after letter to my newspaper Q&A column.

Villagers in ancient China got on relatively well during periods when local gentries brokered relations between commoners and the imperial government. Clan affiliation further determined who did what. There was a sense of order. But social and political disorder has characterized much of Chinese history, including the past two hundred years. Disorder leaves the impression among common people that anything good can be taken away, and that fatalism fosters suspicion of those outside one's tightest circle, the family.

Compounding the get-ahead mindset, the socio-political chaos of the 20th Century and an opaque legal system can make it hard to trust people outside close personal networks. My friends crossing the bridge between university graduation and their first jobs dove straight into their immediate friends and relatives for help finding well-paid, career-related work. Otherwise, some told me, jobs will go to people who already know the hiring manager or who knows someone who knows her or him. More veteran job seekers let me know that some applicants had learned from their parents' grittiness coming off the Cultural Revolution, the Great Famine and other regressive periods of history. Meaning, they threw money and even their naked bodies at employers to get hired — and get ahead instead of falling back.

Religious forces such as those popular in poor Southeast Asian countries, among others, have too little traction in China to promote widespread ethics. Legal barriers to growing charities and pro-social non-profits restrict the kind of NGOs that could help the poor, the inexperienced and under-networked in China. The government exerts so much influence on NGOs that they operate more like mini ministries than groups of organically well-meaning people who have come together to help others.

I looked at multiple definitions of civil society for this chapter and settled on this definition by the Washington-based think tank Center for Strategic & International Studies: a "complex and interconnected network of individuals and groups drawn from rich histories of associational relationships and interactions". Countries with wealth, political stability and legal protections normally have that network. They teem with independent labor unions, charities such as the Salvation Army, service clubs such as Rotary International, a church for every neighborhood and advocacy groups from stray dog shelters to political action committees that lobby legislators. A lot of these groups are founded to advance causes to help segments of society that are weaker than the mainstream. They prove that strangers can help one another instead of just competing.

Part III
School, Work and Money

Education as Raw Material to Get Rich

A woman named Cherry wrote this impassioned letter to my Beijing newspaper advice column:

"I've graduated from a relatively ordinary university," she wrote. "Every conceivable effort was applied toward my first and second majors. In my fourth year, I decided to pursue my master's degree at a key university. But I failed the admission exam because I studied for merely one month and underestimated the competition.

"At that time, while my cousin received her master's degree in Britain, I was encouraged to continue chasing my dream," the letter continues. "I abandoned several other opportunities to prepare for the exam. My maternal grandfather departed from our world forever and my mother had an operation then. But I thought I would at last succeed. However, unbelievably, I failed in one topic. Is this a miserable joke or an absurd mistake?"

It's neither one. Grandfathers, operations and missed opportunities have weight in China as they do anywhere. But education has just as much, maybe more, which is why Cherry followed the cultural norm and did everything she could. Education, for most, is the main conduit to material wealth and, for some, pursued only to get high-paid work.

Classes for high school students stress useful yet ordinary knowledge, rather than arts or sports. Cramming for exams — just ask Cherry — has a way of blocking off a month or more of someone's life except for quick meals and minimal sleep. The serious go-getter will find there's always another exam, say, to prove knowledge of English or accounting, just around the corner, even far into adulthood.

In developed countries, material wealth has penetrated far enough into the population for long enough that most people figure there's some for just about everyone, reducing the get-ahead drive often felt in China.

Copious knowledge of big topics such as math, languages and science translates into high scores on standardized exams, per the prevailing mindset. High scores on university admission exams alone fetch spots in China's top schools. A bachelor's degree or higher from one of those schools, such as Peking University or its neighbor Tsinghua University, leads to far better jobs than their equivalents from more average schools.

In China, it is possible to meet working-class people who are taking a month off work, even quitting a day job, to prepare for a test so they can find a job in something higher-paying, such as finance or accounting.

Lan Min, a Shaanxi Province woman who wrote to my Q&A column, planned to quit a waitressing job because she thought it would eventually pay more to study full time for a test. "My boyfriend persuaded me to give up the job because of its low pay," she wrote. The boyfriend's advice captures the wider sentiment perfectly: "He said I could make use of my free time to acquire knowledge, which would create more wealth," Lan Min writes.

Scholars have formed a distinct, and respected, Chinese

social class since far back into the dynasties. These souls often genuinely care about knowledge for the satisfaction of knowing, or for the catharsis of passing it on to others who take it seriously. Scholars would advise dynastic officials, a reason that the extra well-educated had higher status than common people. But I found as a teacher in Beijing and Taipei that most people who pursue knowledge think more like Cherry. Courses at public schools as well as private ones are usually designed to improve scores on standardized exams such as the ones Cherry took. Whether teaching or just hanging out with friends in Beijing, I was routinely asked as a native English speaker for tips on how to pass the two dominant language-proficiency exams TOEFL (Test of English as a Foreign Language) or IELTS (International English Language Testing System), recognized then by Western universities. The frequency of their questions showed how much they cared about exams — and usually just about reliable ways to pass them rather than mastery of underlying language ability.

One university horticulture major wrote to my column from Chongqing about the possible aftermath of learning purely for the love of knowledge. Right-or-wrong questions about facts, not brain-challenging analytical questions, appeared most often on her exams, she wrote. Her scholarly ambition was eventually soiled. "I like science very much, especially mathematics and physics, so I often go to the physics college to do some experiments. I usually learn science by myself instead of just accepting others' opinions. So, on tests I cannot get very high marks."

The horticulture student's parents wanted her to chase high marks so she could get admitted to a master's program. Mothers and fathers usually pay tuition, so they have a say about what to study, meaning potentially boring majors with the prospect of high-paid jobs. Some parents even decide how often, when and where their university-aged students sit down to study. They're trying to raise the odds of high exam scores.

Education historically has more weight than other criteria—sometimes all the weight—in hiring decisions. Employers may figure that work performance follows naturally from mastery of exam-verified, pre-taught skillsets rather than softer assets such as teamwork and the aptitude for on-the-job learning. Popular employers, due to the high number of applications, may screen applicants by the name recognition of any universities attended and test scores rather than evaluating each applicant's profile.

The tests just keep coming. Chinese university graduates who hope to work in government must pass the popular yet tough civil service exam. People gunning for jobs at foreign companies in China will zero in on passing the TOEIC (Test of English for International Communication), a standardized English test for professionals.

Applicants to overseas postgraduate programs may feel surprised when they must write essays and prove extracurricular activities to get admitted. They're surprised that good exam scores alone were not enough.

The thirst for education doesn't stop at the formal kind. Westerners in China frequently meet people who ask for English lessons either for pay or as a language exchange where the foreigner learns Chinese and no one gets paid. I did five language exchanges over my first couple years in Beijing. English is seen as a ticket to overseas graduate programs as well as jobs in companies where employees are tasked with reading documents from offshore and talking with foreign clients, partners and supervisors. Those companies tend to pay better than average in China, and that matters.

Why English Mastery Is Tough Despite Years of Formal Study

English is an all but compulsory second language in China, but mastery is rare. A Beijing department store once hung signs calling itself a 'monopolistic shop'. A temple complex in the historic district of Datong in Shanxi Province hung a poster years ago saying, "Please visitors be out of bounds," instead of "Keep out". It appears some days that almost every English-language sign in China uses at least one word out of context, spells something incorrectly or flouts the basics of grammar. So many funny, awkward, side-splitting or at least eye-splitting English-language labels turn up in China that some expatriates make a hobby of collecting these gaffes. I admit to having my own small photo collection of mangled language on signs. Travelers with a pile of countries in their passports might grumble that proper spoken English is just as hard to find in China. Airport, hotel and restaurant staffers who speak the language as a work requirement usually know just a short list of job-related phrases. A hotel clerk who waxes fluidly about a key deposit would struggle to answer a friendly question about what he did over the weekend.

Obviously, the millions upon millions who study hard

eventually learn how and those who live overseas speak the global language with expected fluency. The letters to my newspaper column that I keep talking about were 100 percent English and a lot of them were written before internet translators were invented. My first group of Beijing friends was English speakers and I owe their language skills and unearthly willingness to hang out with me to my getting adapted to the city.

But many more — the people who learn because learning is required — regard English more as a job-related tool rather than something purely for knowledge's sake (a coda to Chapter 21). That's the first issue. Second one, teachers often treat foreign languages as science, based on a finite list of rules rather than an ever-changing art form moulded by centuries of daily usage. Then there's the widely held belief that English is inherently simpler than Chinese. Students compare twenty-six alphabet letters to the thousands of Chinese characters. Coming out ahead in East-West cultural comparisons backs up pro-China messages spread through the nation's state-controlled school textbooks and mass media.

Users of English in China want to be right but often don't know how. Written errors typically arise from translating word for word from dictionaries without consulting people who are fluent. They often believe English is a modular language, meaning one that allows for character-by-character mapping into English. Translations of word clusters, from any source language to any destination language, are likely to be more accurate.

Schools in China teach English from primary school through to university, so most people have a chance to learn, though formal education was de-emphasizing the language as of 2024. China is dripping with enthusiasm, too. I found a 2011 poll by one of China's top-ranked universities saying Chinese had overall positive attitudes toward English and felt their country's social norms supported learning it. Many parents send their children to after-school private English lessons, and adults keen to improve their job prospects study English on their own. More adventurous ones approach foreigners in the street for speaking and listening practice. I remember I could go to the Wangfujing pedestrian shopping street in Beijing almost anytime and meet — or, rather be met by — at least a couple of strangers offering free guide service as a way to practice English. Fluency helps open doors to well-paid jobs at foreign-owned companies. All in all, about 200 million people speak some level of English in China, meaning one in every seven. Some fifty million secondary schoolchildren are enrolled in formal English classes.

No small number of Chinese learners do feel a passion for English. They want to know every shortcut, slang phrase and hair-thin difference between American and British versions of the language. Whenever they can speak it, they do. I met dozens of these people as a teacher and journalist. Their drive helped inspire me to carry on with my Chinese studies.

But too many of those who use English for work can't fully operate in the language. Classic is the hotel clerk mentioned above who speaks prolifically about the returning the room key but is at a loss to describe his day off. They often have studied English just for career advancement. These learners fret more over grabbing language certification than over actual proficiency because they figure the proof of learning, not actual fluency, leads to jobs. They're hardly wrong. Certificates lead to admission at overseas graduate schools as well. Tests for these credentials are weighted toward reading, writing and listening skills, not speaking. Special preparation books help people pass the tests by anticipating the questions rather than getting their overall English skills up to a testable level.

Language is taught in the typical school in China much

as math and science is taught, meaning rote memorization. Traditional teachers might suppose that after enough years of memorizing words and patterns, a student will burn vocabulary and basic grammar into the brain's language centers, which will in turn reproduce it flawlessly. Classroom instruction in China often omits drills that would give students chances to hear and speak the language in its raw, non-textbook form. It's no surprise so many Chinese can write passable English yet barely speak it.

Teachers play up memorization because words and phrases appear on China's standardized exams. Instructors may be evaluated for competency based on the median exam scores for their classes. I knew one public school teacher, a young enthusiastic one who started out believing in English as an organically cool language, but whose job was threatened if her students didn't reach a certain average score on a district-wide exam. University-level exams cover reading comprehension and composition of basic sentences. High schoolers need neither speak English nor understand spoken English to pass.

One student once wrote to my newspaper column that "when we were in high school, we only did some English papers to increase our scores and seldom focused on our oral English, (and) while in university, especially for an English major, I found that my oral English is so poor that whenever I open my mouth the teacher would say 'no'."

Despite the 2011 poll, some Chinese still look down on English. I discovered this viewpoint through chats with friends and through an opinion piece on *The People's Daily* website: "English actually isn't a complete language," the piece says. "In truth, English is easier to study than Chinese, and in the process of grasping vocabulary the demand from English is much less."

I took an international linguisticss course at my own university and did some follow up internet research for this chapter. The scholars generally believe that one language is as complex as the next as long as the fluent can effectively communicate any possible idea about every possible topic. Chinese does that job. English does, too.

Why Hands Don't Get Raised at Meetings

Something keeps chilling group discussion in China. A teacher might ask her class to call out a three-letter word that starts with 'd' and refers to a common household pet. Everyone knows. Let's say no one answers. Now let's say the teacher goes on to pick someone at random from the student roster to state his English name. After a few seconds of stammering, the student clears his throat and speaks in a voice that the teacher can barely hear. Exaggeration? I confess. But I've taught in China and moments like these do occur.

Boardrooms, aside from a couple of senior people who do most of the talking, are usually as quiet as these classrooms, even if the multiple staff people privately have a list of rich and useful things to say. I went to meetings of this type at a news agency in Taiwan where I worked for more than four years. When a department head calls everyone in the office to an impromptu meeting, probably once again few people speak.

The quiet ones usually fear a backlash for anything said out of turn. They hope to avoid humiliation at the hands of teachers, meeting organizers and supervisors in case they make a statement, even a well-meaning one, which conveys misinformation or any hint of a challenge to management. Thanks to a tradition of obedience, many in China withhold all but the most upbeat, congratulatory ideas in formal meetings with superiors. Happy authorities ensure people under them get key rewards — grades, income, another spot on the board — instead of getting chastised or someday sacked over an offense.

Back in elementary school, lots of these obsequious college students and employees would shoot their hands into the air when teachers asked questions. They wanted to show off knowledge to the class and relieve nerves that grew antsy from sitting at a desk so long. I've seen those hands waving in the air like palms on a beach when volunteering as a story reader in elementary schools. Yet most of these ten-year-olds will keep their hands down by the time they're eighteen, even though they still have knowledge and want to impress teachers. Some people do continue to speak fluidly in classrooms and meeting rooms. They're not quite outliers but far from a majority.

A second-year international business major named Jade once wrote to my newspaper Q&A column that she considered public speaking an 'important skill' but said, "I always think what I said in public is not good, and I fear that someone will laugh at me."

People in any country know the fear of derision, especially if they're struggling to keep up with instructions and feel surrounded by more tuned-in peers. They know a department head could answer a question about company policy by admonishing the employee to re-read the in-house website. The website may or may not offer a firm answer to the question. One person getting pounced on like that will deter others in the room from raising their own hands.

In China, there's more. A conventional teacher doesn't

always believe the Western truism that there is no such thing as a stupid question. Too many conventional leaders in China expect their charges to absorb information letter for letter, number for number, as presented, without discussion. Teachers who think this way naturally come down hard on wrong answers. As the State University of New York's Buffalo campus once said in a presentation to prepare its faculty for Chinese students, per a document I found online, "Traditionally, teachers (in China) view themselves as distributors of previous knowledge, not facilitators of learning process." By middle school, students recognize the teachers who are rigid distribution channels and avoid in-class comments that might get in the way.

Students who normally keep quiet risk being judged almost entirely on the few comments they do make, because what other criteria are there? Harsher teachers use the sum of each student's comments to label the learner, openly, as an introvert, extrovert, muddle-head or, on the more flattering side, the lookalike of some famous person. My core teacher at Peking University handed out labels like those to our class of foreign learners of basic Mandarin. Fear of the teacher's snap evaluation motivates no small number of students to ask one another, not the teacher, to explain concepts that they didn't follow in class. Peer-to-peer chatter after staff meetings clears up questions that no one dared ask the supervisor.

Where questions border on challenges, supervisors and instructors may feel outright offended. They wouldn't be used to these queries, assuming rather that everything said is clear from the outset. Instead of saying, "Great question, I'll get back to you," teachers in China are likely to question the question. These comebacks emphasize what social sciences call 'power distance', a term I learned in a communication studies master's program. A humorless, quick-to-criticise teacher who at the same time appears knowledgeable on a subject exudes enough counter-mojo to stop students from raising questions. The teacher is using power to add distance.

Power distance explains why company meetings, especially when run by stern bosses, move quickly due to a lack of discussion. Bigger conferences can take on the aura of a pep rally. For example, during the SARS respiratory disease outbreak around China in 2003, I covered an event where hundreds of white-uniformed doctors and nurses stood outside a major Beijing hospital listening to a leader from inside lecture about how to stay safe. Not a single white sleeve in the audience went up with a question, even though medical workers faced more risk of dying than peers in any other profession and no one knew then quite how to treat SARS, while dodging the disease itself. It's hard to imagine no one had questions.

Lack of queries in these settings helps whoever is in a position of authority to stay there. Subjects' willingness to keep quiet under someone's rule, whether or not they agree with how it's carried out, have supported multiple millennia of single-party or single-dynasty rule in China.

Too many right answers, especially if given voluntarily, build up a rank-and-filer as the too-tall blade of grass that needs to be cut down so everyone in the room is equal. The blade of grass is a common Chinese metaphor used in cases where someone tries to stand out, even when fully entitled to try. The one who is right threatens to command too many resources as a taller blade would do to the surrounding soil. The resource in a classroom would be passing grades that are generated by a known formula and threatened by one among them who raises the bar by excelling in front of a teacher. Statements from the ranks in a boardroom threaten to trim the power distance of a CEO if they're better argued or convey more recent data. The threatened CEO could target the hand-raiser later, denying that person some kind of reward.

Why A-Plus University Students Miss China's Best Jobs

Chinese society, like any other, values students with high marks. Parents usually pay university tuition and expect a return on that money in the form of top exam scores. Up through a child's high school years, Mom and Dad might even punish children who don't bring home good scores. But I taught journalism in Beijing to a man who missed a slew of classes and received a class score in the 60s. He went on to get a big-time foreign media job while several of his classmates with scores 30 points higher floundered about after graduation for half a year pondering whether to pursue master's degrees. One guy whom I taught later at the same school racked up attendance and scores that were just as shoddy. He got hired as a videographer with a well-paying, international news agency that sent him on top-drawer assignments. His two front-row, A-level classmates? Grad school and low-paid civil service jobs, because that was all they could get. The best jobs in China, with chilling frequency, don't go to students with the highest marks.

Students with A's often lack the social experience that builds connections and crucial savvy about the work world. They're studying too hard in many cases to hang out, especially if their parents require those long hours with homework and exam review notes. The best jobs in China often go to people with personal connections, skill in finding positions that aren't widely advertised and mastery of job interviews. Prime jobs in lots of countries swing the same way, but students in China believe more fervently than peers outside that grades are supposed to matter. Students with a social network, from a boyfriend to an internship, are more likely than their over-studied classmates to learn these unwritten rules of the job hunt and find their way to a position. They might even have made those connections by skipping weeks of classes — as my student who scored in the 60s did — and begging professors for the passing score (he didn't beg).

Grades do carry weight in China's job market, as do exam scores, as noted in Chapter 21. A fresh graduate probably wouldn't apply against fifty other people for an urban white-collar job with scores in the sixties unless she or he had a surefire connection in the employer's management and most people lack inside connections at primo companies. Due to China's size and traditional emphasis on scores over other qualifications, lots of people study hard for stellar grades. The problem is, employers who feel fatigued by so many high scores tend to take shortcuts, which is where an applicant's connections and dazzling job interviews come in. Universities seldom teach these skills along with math, sciences and languages.

Tuition-paying parents may recall their own twenties, in an era before private enterprise was so widespread, when applicants with top grades and high standardized exam scores got the best paid, most stable jobs. That was before China's economy stratified away from just farming, manufacturing and state jobs into foreign-owned firms, a full-on financial sector and one of the world's top IT employment hubs. Chinese schools from K-through-MBA focus heavily on grades, too, largely because there were fewer spots open on China's campuses. Elders don't always realize that their son with a composite 60 score and a vast social network is more likely to get hired today than the top scorer in his class who spent most of his free time in the library. They might believe instead in the traditional, practical Chinese idea that the right hardware, rather than soft social skills, brings the best results. In education, hardware means that proof of superior book knowledge should open any door. Chinese schools and universities focus on book knowledge anyhow.

These parents in turn pressure their children to sit in the university classroom's front rows, take copious notes and study relentlessly for exams. Teachers like me love them because they're punctual, quiet and attentive, rather than making us wonder why they've been absent all of, say, October. Occupants of the front rows are less likely to deviate from their studies into dating, part-time work or karaoke. Those studying in their hometowns live at home instead of in a university dormitory room, eliminating the risk of distraction by hanging out with friendly roommates.

At government-run China Central Television, a popular employer in Beijing, superstar young reporters often find openings through friends and get hired by exuding confidence during job interviews. I heard about this route to employment from my many journalism students who ended up working at the network.

Applicants with social skills find chatting with an employer more natural than do their rivals who had focused mainly on class attendance and exam preparation. They're used to interacting with company managers, campus club heads and just friends. The socially skilled don't sweat during a job interview over sharing personal information other than their grades. Top-scoring students may try to get hired solely by sending resumes and telling employers about their scores, but then come off as nervous in interviews.

After the grade-A students do get jobs, they may struggle to advance or even hold their positions in workplaces where social finessing is required to get promotions and crucial assignments. I've heard friend after friend use the term 'subtle relationships' among colleagues to describe this kind of struggle. Much of the subtlety comes down to new hires treating certain equals as de facto superiors. A newly graduated university student named Rose put it like this in her letter to my Beijing newspaper column, "I was dismissed after a probation period, and to my surprise the reason was that I'm too quiet. Though I'm an introverted girl, I had strong responsibilities. I worked hard and carefully, even doing extra work, yet failed." A more sociable, less studious Rose may have known how to build relations and avoid being kicked out.

Dreams, Decisions and Demons that Divide Them

Chinese youth stand apart from plenty of their peers overseas for sacrificing personal passions in favor of more practical, less interesting jobs. Twenty-somethings in this category probably won't be cutting any travel videos even if they like film more than any other field. They wouldn't go to art school overseas despite a penchant for painting. More likely, people in this conservative bandwidth of China get degrees in the hard sciences and business-related disciplines with jobs later to match.

The cancellation of dreams usually comes down to money. Elders, who often control family budgets, may steer their grown children away from fields such as arts, sports and charity work because of poor pay compared to jobs in science or business. Families of this type would expect all wage earners to contribute income for the support of all, as explained in Chapter 13. Chinese people are more prosperous now, but legal and systemic opacity makes many wonder how long their wealth will hold out, so they go where the money is surest.

In some families, particularly well-off urban ones, children may end up with multi-colored hair, a thing for punk rock and degrees in the arts from schools in Western Europe. Their peers from this segment of society have become China's new generation of app developers and boutique hotel operators. Children in the family may play video games or surf online sites rather than study relentlessly, so they know it's technically possible to do what they freely want as adults. I met a Beijing woman, Diana Jone, years ago who embodied this ideal: learned English on her own because she felt like it, followed her own sense of fashion and tweaked her surname to sound more Anglo. Her parents didn't mind, she told me, convincingly (because she never talked about arguments at home). She worked in a bakery and a private school before co-founding a firm that organizes international homestays.

Diana still heads up a growing minority, but still a minority. Studious undergraduates from China's countryside and lower-tier cities sometimes can barely afford meals with their classmates, let alone a degree from Europe. Their parents may have saved up tuition, room and board for years even at the expense of their own basic well-being. These families put so much into a child's university education that they expect a highly productive outcome. A new university graduate whose lower middle-class parents have paid four to six years of tuition probably find it hard to protest what Mom and Dad want in a career.

A woman wrote this letter to my newspaper Q&A column ten years after her university graduation: "Like other Chinese children who follow in their parents' footsteps, I majored in the same field that my parents chose, and I didn't like it at all. In recent years, I've tired of the job. I have other knowledge that has nothing to do with my work, but I'm not into it. I feel lost."

Parents in their fifties upward usually didn't dream about their own adult lives because they couldn't. A lot were assigned jobs under communism 1.0. Money was a crushing concern because families once had much less of it. People from this background easily worry that today's accumulation of wealth, if stolen or suddenly missing, would fall below the radar of police or courts, because those mechanisms have long been weak in China. High-paid, stable jobs for their children assuage concerns about income. A grown child's interest in arts, sports or high-tech startups—all regarded as risky and low-paid—would fan the concerns. The epitome of stability is a government desk job, even if it pays less than the private sector. Women may be lobbied at home to become K-12 schoolteachers, a type of public servant considered by many traditional Chinese to be right for a woman.

Against these demands, youth might feel guilty working in a bakery or launching a homestay operation. They might be thinking: our extended family could need money at any time and I'm about to become a breadwinner. My parents have supported me through the university years and want to retire. Will they get sick then and need more money for healthcare? Mom keeps saying to take the civil service exam. I don't want to work in government, stable as the job may be. My degree in English has no relation to civil service. I majored in English because I wanted to work in television overseas. That's my ideal."

Their ambition takes another step back when it feels like everyone else on campus is taking the civil service exam and e-mailing resumes to major companies about office administrative jobs—moderately skilled positions that are also seen as stable. Against this tide, new graduates may even wonder why they ever really had unconventional career ideas.

The focus on lucrative work shows too among ethnic Chinese people outside China. Americans marvel, for example, at how many people of Chinese descent hold engineering and healthcare jobs and wonder why relatively few work, for example, in local journalism.

When dreams are realized, they often follow a series of tough cross-generation arguments. The young adults might prevail because of friends who are following their own dreams, offering a counterweight to family pressure. A peer who has already set up a business, for example, and earns enough income to hire her friends becomes a particularly strong magnet—especially if someone bickering with family elders can land a job with her.

One fourth-year Chinese university student sent this story to my column. "At the moment, my parents want me to be a teacher, but I don't like that option," she wrote. "During my holiday break, I worked part time as a tour guide in my hometown. I like the job very much. But my parents don't agree with me. I always consider what my parents say, but it's hard for me to make a decision." Tour guide salaries vary in China and workloads fluctuate wildly, such as to near demise during the Covid-19 pandemic. Teaching is the solid opposite.

Years later, a safe career job may quickly grow dull. People do grow into non-dream jobs if they get along with colleagues, earn steady income and find proud parents on home visits. Marriage and childcare provide life stimulus that the job lacks. But those who still feel an unrequited career dream keep wondering what they gave up. They could quit and chase the dream again, but that route would probably require a socially awkward return to school at an age ten to twenty years older than most students. It could require relocating and a cut in the income that supports their children and aging parents. Unrequited dreamers more often comfort themselves with the idea that they're safe even if unsatisfied.

Money Handlers, not Shopkeepers

A caffeine-reliant Beijinger should be happy to discover a coffeehouse just opened in the neighborhood. It would serve beans of the day from Africa and the Americas. There would be free WiFi and a quiet corner for laptop sessions. But more likely than not, after a few months of business, a building renovation crew would suddenly occupy the space. A hair salon would move in a few weeks later and outlive the cafe because overhead requires just rent, cheap labor and a few tools, while customers could pay $50 to $100 per visit, much more than a cup of coffee. Cafes don't offer fast, easy money. Salons are in a league with China's breeders of prized birds and dogs. They prosper too because of low overhead and high prices. Same for art dealers. Agency work is fantastically popular in China too. I've met my share of people who run 'cultural exchange companies', which they'll eventually explain means helping set up high-participation industry conferences that charge steep fees for wealthy exhibitors.

A single theme unites these ventures: they are founded on a plan to make money quickly at low cost. The advice, "Do what you love, and the money will follow," with which I grew up in the United States, earns little sympathy in China. The wait for money to follow, if it really does, fails to feed a family over the next half year. A post-poverty psychology in China pushes people into these short-term business ventures — and right out of them as soon as income starts to taper off.

Naturally, with a population as big as China's, plenty of entrepreneurs open shops because they care about their wares: coffee, fitness, fountain pens and musical instruments, to name a few examples from Beijing. These operators are willing to wait. They advertise. They market. They redo the business plan as needed to find customers. Merchants, craftspeople and performers realise happy customers return, spend more money and make referrals to friends. It just takes *some time*.

But the quest for quick money remains the gold standard. It arises from a historical thirst to achieve a better life, which makes the need for fast money especially acute. Today businesspeople do their best (or worst) to let proceeds pile up within a few months. Chinese were among the world's earliest people to mint money, giving the society early exposure to duplication as a source of wealth.

Accentuating this trend, wealth is never totally safe, either. To whom would the jilted turn for help? National leaders over the centuries tend to ignore day-to-day troubles affecting commoners unless the state too is impacted. That means a money dispute between two commoners comes down in most cases to one person's bullheadedness or a spirit of compromise — rather than on intervention by police or courts. In a lot of cases, the jilted just mutter "mei banfa" (no way this will work) and accept the loss.

Lack of government oversight has allowed China's shadow-banking sector to challenge regulators in the 21st Century. Shadow banking refers to groups of unregistered people who lend money and accept deposits for investment purposes. These schemes disrupt the predictable flows of capital, a vague threat to broader economic stability, but officials lack the mandate or capacity to examine every exchange of money in such a big country.

Civil lawsuits are relatively rare if held up to China's 1.4 billion population and an incalculable number of scams. Filing a lawsuit involves a reel of red tape, and judges are sometimes known to favor whichever litigant is higher status, say a major business owner or a party official, regardless of what actually went wrong. Welfare and socialized healthcare remain shaky despite constant headway, meaning many people still expect to pay their own expenses when jobless or sick.

The better schools in China's higher education system admit just high school students with the top exam scores. Most test takers get ordinary scores, meaning technical school or blue-collar work that requires no formal schooling. Blue-collar jobs seldom pay well, and they can easily cause injury from overwork. In China, people may feel ashamed if they work with their hands, unlike blue-collar people in Western countries who take pride in (and earn decent money from) drywalling, sheetrocking and repairing cars. These professionals in the West even get union protection and social respect.

The quick turnover of money with minimal hard work now offers a chance for common Chinese to ensure income in a grey society and escape blue-collar jobs.

MBAs have bloomed only over the past two decades. A lot of businesspeople lack a long-term development goal, a clear target market and the savings to survive a slow start before any profit.

Small entrepreneurs in China traditionally have what an International Labor Organization project leader described to me as a 'household economy' mentality toward money management. That meant massing income throughout the week, spending most of it on expenses by Sunday and saving the rest, then starting all over on Monday. The alternative would be to reinvest a lot of that Monday-Friday income in the startup's product or service. The ILO had taken me to Inner Mongolia to report on its project giving technical aid to lower-income female heads of households who wanted to start their own businesses but lacked experience managing their ledgers.

In this spirit, agency work such as property sales and third-party job recruiting have more appeal than creating one's own goods or services. I've lived in neighborhoods where literally every third storefront belongs to a property agency. Their sales of apartments can fetch a massive commission from a single buyer after a few meetings. No hard physical labor is involved. Chinese cities with foreign business communities support a disproportionate number of self-employed language translators, as that line of work favors duplication over creation and someone with top skills can get it done fast.

At beauty salons, young migrants from the countryside accept low wages for cutting, shaving and dying hair. The salon operator can handily profit as people are willing to pay a lot to change their looks.

Gaps in China's customer service, a part of doing business that can be time-consuming with little immediate reward, reflect the drive for quick money over any long-term effort to build client relations. Clerks in some places seldom smile or greet customers unless they come ready to plop down a pile of cash, I found everywhere from corner markets to department stores. They might give terse answers to difficult customer questions rather than eagerly getting to the heart of what a customer is asking for and chasing down an answer. I found these regressive chats most common on the phone. I would call to ask whether something was in stock—and if not, I'd be told "no" rather than,

"We'll get back to you next month when our new inventory comes in." Sometimes customers can't find any help because the service staffers are in a backroom having a smoke and a WeChat session.

The thirst for fast money plus the spottiness of law enforcement has led some business operators to crime. Shadow banking is one example. Translators might steal reports from the internet and turn the material around in Chinese without consent from the creators. In 2022, an English-language news reporter colleague of mine pulled up a full version of a feature story she wrote as republished in a Chinese-language newspaper, which gave her no credit. Around 2000, factories earned a bit of their income from assembly lines that burned DVDs for sale on the black market, without permission from a single film studio. Few people in these trades are doing quite what they love, especially against the risk of getting caught, but they're holding off financial desperation and the need to do blue-collar work.

Big Brother, Little Sister: Workplace Relations

A male office worker once confessed to me he could not see his younger female co-worker as his equal. Another one, new to his job, wondered in a letter to my newspaper Q&A column why his superiors never talk to him. A newsroom intern said in another letter she was bewildered that someone else's name appeared on a story she wrote. These vignettes speak to the difficulties experienced in Chinese workplaces. Employees the world over work with lazy or arrogant people here and there. But in China, there's all that plus another layer of relationships that employees often call so 'complex' that discussion about these dynamics rules out many after-hours gatherings among friends.

In most cases, sticky co-worker relations arise from a lack of detailed in-house chain-of-command rules made clear to all employees and followed at all ranks. But, in most cases, an informal, culturally defined hierarchy determined by age, rank and gender fill that void.

Company rules on who's supposed to do what, wherever in the world these codes exist, form a contract between managers and the managed. The managed know what's expected and in turn aim to succeed at work by following the rules.

At a typical company in China, though of course not all of them, a few people at the top run things based on unspoken understandings with their staff members. Adding to confusion in the ranks, the higher-ups might not have job-related titles such as chief technology officer or procurement manager.

Survival in a company with few to no clear rules means outdoing fellow staff members in anticipating a supervisor's needs and serving them. That's where relations get complex. When everyone is trying to psych out the same boss, especially a busy and uncommunicative one, the office spawns a quiet but rigorous competition for raises, promotions, prime assignments and performance recognition. It won't usually be in the employee handbook, if there is one. Instead, each employee seeks a special relationship with the bosses to ensure delivery of whatever makes them happy. In extreme cases, maintenance of those relations takes gifts, meals outside work time and sexual favors. But usually, supervisors just like some people more than others because certain workers make management duties easier. Company heads may even favor these people over harder-working peers who are more distant and less cognizant of the little things that make supervisors comfortable—from getting the coffee to taking calls from problem clients.

Chinese people have long operated under strong leaders, from an authoritarian parent to the country's emperor or president. These rulers are known for acting autonomously rather than through checks and balances that would include living by a latticework of rules on how underlings perform. Authority in China is seldom challenged openly. Ideally, leaders know what they are doing and treat people under them responsibly. That's a tenet of Confucianism, a Chinese code respected by society because it has offered order to a sometimes politically and economically chaotic country for 2,500 years.

Today's company heads may further realize that a lack of strict guidelines allows them maximum flexibility in finding clients and making major investments at top speed.

Back to our opening vignettes, the Beijing-based intern at a Beijing news media outlet contacted my newspaper Q&A column about a shock to her work relations. "When I wrote a piece of news and finally found my writing on the front page with the name of another, experienced journalist, I was deeply hurt, but none of my colleagues think this is a big deal," the writer, named Shelley, said.

She was right out of a university and assumed the company would follow widespread international practice in the media, where writers get their own names published. But news media in China are less strict. Some reports are copied not only from interns but also from other media, ideally though not always with permission. If Shelly was to buddy up to one of the assigning editors, her name might show up more often. She might even get to leave the newsroom at the standard 5:30 p.m. quitting time and take weekends off instead of working odd hours on breaking news stories.

Disillusioned workers tend to get on better too by fitting into an unspoken system best described as big brother, little sister. Many older men assume de facto authority unless ranks are otherwise spelled out, which they're usually not, except for the top management. Younger women in this setting would normally have the least clout and older women rank above junior men. This Chinese social hierarchy has evolved over the centuries, so most modern company workers viscerally get it — even if it they personally find it outdated and unfair. The dynamic goes back to traditional agrarian family values — Chinese as well as global — that prize age and the male gender.

The videographer referenced above, twenty-nine years old at the time, said he could not see his twenty-three-year-old female producer in 'any other way' than as a younger sister who needed guidance. She happened to earn more money than he did and speak better English, a core job skill. The company's big bosses from overseas saw her as their go-to person in the office.

They were hired at the same time. Had he started before her, as an older male employee, he might have turned into her de facto supervisor. Men who do have that head start in a company would know it better than newbies and understand what the busy real boss is thinking. This male colleague wanted his younger hires to tap him for guidance and take any suggestions rather than competing with his views.

Not uncommonly, more than one man in the company will vie for this biggest brother role. Rivalry over who's got better advice and who's closer to the real boss can create infighting that forces lower-ranking people to take sides. And not everyone agrees that the gender-slash-age hierarchy should apply to a modern workplace. Resentment among the younger, female employees is likely to grow from passive grumbling to outbreaks of defiance as they gain experience in the company. Some will quit their jobs.

A man on the job for one year wrote this description to my Q&A column of the subtle and complex relations in his office with few formal rules. "My colleague (an older man, rising star) does not want to talk to me. Maybe he is too arrogant. He looks down upon others who are under his position. I have tried to improve our office atmosphere but unsuccessfully. My colleagues can bear this tedium, and he does not pay much attention to me when I talk to him actively. He just wants to talk to our department manager and our boss. He wants to show he is more capable than us."

Everyone Wants to Be the Boss and Here's How They Do It

People seize power in the most unlikely places. One driver on a team of three equals at a news agency where I once worked found a way to take the easiest jobs with the plushest vehicles. A man running the audio-visual room at a university where I taught set his own hours outside the campus-wide norm and turned people away at other times. Parking garage guards sometimes shoo people off sidewalks, without city permission, to command a bit of space for private vehicles emerging from an underground lot.

The search for power is a universal human habit. After all, the late American psychologist William Glasser's 'choice theory' of human needs ranks 'power' and 'significance' as people's No. 3 agenda item in life after survival and love.

But many Chinese seek power with such unusual persistence that the country teems with de facto leaders in unlikely places such as the A-V room. Power is extra significant in China because lots of people excel in the same conventional ways across a large population. That population size means leaders have more respect than ever, by the sheer numbers, influence more people and control more resources. A history of on-again, off-again weak leadership at all levels of society leaves a lot of authority roles void too, meaning an opportunity to bid for power is seldom far off.

I've never felt qualified for those voids as an outsider in China, so I researched the topic and found Geert Hofstede, a Dutch author and professor who specializes in cultural values. He argues that Chinese citizens accept that not all individuals are equal, and for that reason it hardly matters *why* someone has authority over a given setting. For that reason, and I suspect to keep harmony, workplace colleagues often just throw their trust behind a superior's proven day-by-day ability to lead even if they privately wonder how the person suddenly took control.

Leaders—among chauffeurs or in parking garages for example—in turn pick up on that trust as people around them respect their orders. That's quite a head rush for someone stuck in otherwise static or unrewarding work.

The most fortunate authorities get hired or elected. They have titles and salaries to match. But applications for those positions are hyper-competitive in a country so big and with so many candidates. High-ranking people get hired a lot based on connections rather than proven leadership skills, too, a trend that disillusions other would-be applicants. For these reasons, people who want authority are more likely to pounce on power voids created by weak titular leaders before someone else does.

When the Republic of China replaced the Qing Dynasty after 1911, for example, it couldn't bring the whole country under its control. The new rulers were inexperienced and allowed for the rise of warlords who ran parts of China without deferring to the republic.

As Chapter 27 explains, someone in even the smallest workplaces might bid for de facto authority by building special relations with the real bosses. Workers in dull, low-status jobs bid all the harder because they want the dramatic boost that authority confers.

The driver whom I mentioned used the better of two black sedans, chauffeured the boss around, cherry-picked other assignments and gave the other two drivers orders. The other two went along because they were more recent hires and wanted to keep peace. The office's big boss didn't care, as long as he got driven to where he wanted to go. Building guards have no legal authority over the streets, where passing vehicles have a legal right of way, but they still flag their hands 'stop' and blow whistles so their own tenants can come and go. At the audio-visual room, the man with his own hours grew famous among students for picking at his convenience when he felt like opening the door and rebuffing equipment rental requests that he found too complicated. He had created rules all his own.

I got around the A-V guy's stylized rules by asking my own supervisor to intervene for me, which she did. The senior driver would give me rides only if authorized first by more senior people in the bureau. His two colleagues just said, "Let's go," if their schedules allowed.

Leaders like these confuse outsiders who are looking for the right person in an organization to get something done. An outsider focused on formal ranks and titles will naturally overlook a common staff member who can authorise a transaction. Outsiders irritated by poor customer service in China might have just stepped into too many workplaces where people spend more hours on the job seeking to expand their scope of control than on satisfying clients.

Power-seekers such as the audio-video room keeper and the driver tend to be middle-aged to older people who understand every detail of how their workplaces operate, a requirement for taking de facto control. They are well positioned to scan for hidden portals to power. Is the real boss gone a lot or uninterested in daily routines? Do I have the only set of keys, or an unrivaled skillset? Perfect: make up new rules and see what happens.

Men do an outsized share of the power grabbing. As a man who never grabbed any power, I'll quote from Tom Doctoroff's book *Billions: Selling to the New Chinese Consumer*. He says a man in China should be 'successful' at age thirty and 'have no doubt' about himself by forty. The path to those two milestones was more uniform before China became richer, more urban and more economically stratified after the 1980s. Men now face what Doctoroff calls the 'anxiety of disorientation'. Because they're not confident in their future, men look for pedestals of power that exude success beyond a doubt.

Women traditionally derive power through long-term accumulation of wealth and management of daily household affairs. This type of authority is all but assured because the home is theirs, not so subject to outside forces. Unless they're vying for control in a vast household of extended family, women may feel less pressure than men to take more power than the household in front of them.

Self-proclaimed authority can stop as fast as it starts. Back to my review of the literature, a shipping company executive with twenty years in China wrote in an article for the management consultancy McKinsey & Company that "leadership is a contact sport" because "everything is personal." The article's author, Nandani Lynton, added, "Managers in China need to pay more personal attention to staff and colleagues than managers in many other cultures do."

For this reason, people such as the A-V room man and the senior driver must focus attentively on preserving their authority. They might, in extreme cases, pay someone off. Some share the authority to neutralize rivals. Those rivals could otherwise rat them out for taking power, and then grab the power themselves — whatever it takes for the highest-order of achievement after survival and love.

Why Employees Work Overtime Even When the Work is Done

In China's major cities, office workers commonly ignore the clock when it strikes 5:30 p.m. and they're legally, contractually allowed to go home. They might pass through their big, automated doorways onto the giant plazas of their towers at 7:00 or 8:00 p.m. instead. Some will head to a metro station for a train home. Others will go back to their desks after a fast bowl of restaurant noodles. I've seen these evenings unfold in Shanghai, Taipei and Hong Kong. I've walked into offices myself after 9:00 p.m. to get something I forgot and to my surprise found a colleague as well as my missing stuff.

Quitting times trend late in workplaces where the most senior person in the office is crazy about his job. That will happen especially if he's part owner of the company. Some supervisors require long hours by calling snap meetings in the evening or handing people new, urgent assignments just minutes before 5:30 p.m. It's hard to leave work until the supervisor puts an obvious end to the day by declaring no further business until tomorrow. A supervisor needn't always be so explicit, either. Workers often impose long hours on themselves to look, in the face of managers and colleagues, as though they care about the company.

This schism between posted and actual quitting times comes down to a quick three-point office memo: point one is the psychology of accumulation. Second is the idea that more hours mean more productivity, a game of pure quantity rather than quality. Third, a culture of loyalty keeps employees on the job for long hours even if it harms their health.

On the accumulation front, a person's worth in China is typically measured by the number of visible material achievements. Total number of hours worked is a measurable achievement. I worked for three years with an ethnic Chinese woman who put in two extra hours many evenings to answer e-mails, wowing someone with the fact it was sent at 7:30 p.m. instead of 5:30 p.m. Employee evaluations based on client feedback, contributions to a company's income and other quality-of-service indicators matter, too. But they're less clear-cut than the sheer observable number of hours that someone clocks. As noted in Chapter 8, the psychology of accumulation explains too why children are urged to spend long days of study to cram knowledge.

Supervisors figure that someone who works ten hours per day in front of a computer will accomplish more than someone who spends just eight hours and it's possible they're right. But the eight-hour worker might have done a more efficient job by making better, faster decisions throughout the workday and avoiding wasted time on minor administrative items. An eight-hour worker is statistically more likely to get more brain rest at home, compared to colleagues who stayed late, and she or he is able to arrive at work more alert the next day.

The quest for accumulation is related to China's history of competition for scarce resources. Plenty of people do see the value of efficiency, time for relaxation and the benefits of a work-life balance. But competition for resources persists now as before—though the resources have shifted from life's basics to high-income jobs and slots in key schools.

Face is another reason for China's emphasis on number of hours worked. Face means a lot of things but in this case simply says: what you see is what you get and don't look past the surface. From this view, one who appears to be working hard by putting in the hours must in fact be working that hard. A worker who wears a blazer and freshly ironed trousers looks even more serious, regardless of what actually gets done by the brain, hands and PC.

Smart, analytical bosses, of course, evaluate hard work along dimensions other than hours spent. What about, for instance, the quality of a worker's output after eight hours compared to ten? At a prominent high-tech firm in Taipei, a mid-level manager told me in a news interview about work-life balance he had suddenly resigned at age forty-nine due to weariness from work and missing out on time with family. He ended up co-managing a smaller tech company where the owner broke ranks with the norm and strictly required the whole staff to leave at 5:00 p.m. Both were Taiwan natives and initially steeped in the culture of overtime.

Not everyone stays late at work. Beijing dwellers including supervisors unabashedly head home at 5:30 p.m. Beijing as the capital is full of government workers, meaning relatively low pressure to stay late and arrange that final money-making deal of the day. The China offices of foreign-owned companies generally encourage clocking out on time.

Loyalty is the third reason for free overtime. Employees typically leave only after their duty supervisor gets off work. Employees tend to stay until the boss leaves to show respect, consciously or otherwise, for the firm's business successes as well as for the supervisor who sees a chronically busy office as a sign of progress and commitment. Supervisors may reinforce this ethos by criticizing staffers who leave around the posted quitting time—often indirectly by complimenting a peer who works longer hours.

But the average employee, I've found, thinks less about a vengeful supervisor than about the almost parent-to-child relationship she or he has with the same person: a purveyor of rewards and punishments. Most sanguine supervisors see themselves as providers. Their employees in turn should see themselves as dutiful children who naturally want to show filial piety. My first Beijing employer, *China Daily*, took the foreign editors on daylong outings around Beijing. Coaches shuttled us around. Admission to parks was paid for. Lunches were on the company. Who wouldn't want to spend a bit more time at work to make a boss happy?

Wage earners who work overtime, incidentally, seldom collect more than eight hours of daily wages despite their contractual and legal rights. What would a demanding, loyalty-conscious boss say about requests for extra pay? To avoid finding out, workers linger. Unlucky ones get assigned complex, time-consuming tasks at 5:30 p.m. Many more just quasi-work a few more hours after 5:30 p.m. and do their own thing online during frequent, furtive breaks. Colleagues chat and build bonds. The better bosses order dinner for everyone who's around, evidence of their family-style provider roles. A formal complaint about overtime pay would poison this familial atmosphere. It would suggest lack of loyalty to company and the family.

Why It's Acceptable to Copy Without Permission

It's hard to be sure what a true original in China is. Pirated software was once so prevalent the government—at times pressured by foreign diplomats to stiffen copyright protection rules—has acknowledged using it in its own offices. The International Federation of the Phonographic Industry told me during a news interview that music copyright violations in China are the worst in the world. Earlier-model Xiaomi-brand smartphones have been widely described as iPhone lookalikes. Untold numbers of Chinese university students have explained to me they paste blocks of copy from copyrighted internet documents into their own term papers without changing the words.

Copycatting is top dog in China, despite enforcement binges following complaints by foreign governments and trade associations about intellectual property violations, because most people don't regard the act as as illegal or immoral. Historical respect for a work's creator and recent political-economic pressure to get ahead materially explain this enduring facet of China. For others, duplication simply means a safe way of creating content.

Copying as a way of life goes back at least 2,500 years, I found in the literature. Chinese writers have long seen re-penning other people's texts as simple transmission of commonly accepted facts and a bow of respect to the people who first transcribed those points. If something is widely considered true, why shouldn't it be repeated and reused for one's own good? Harvard University East Asian Legal Studies director William Alford calls copying a 'transformative engagement' with the past, meaning the past is shared and therefore it's unnecessary to call it private property. Copying of music and books today often still conveys respect for the source, hardly an effort to cheat it, and reflects that sense of a shared past.

Links between duplication and a shared past go back to when the revered scholar Confucius was alive around 500 BC. I didn't grow up around this man's teachings, so I stuck with the literature: Confucius acknowledged in his most famous treatise that he had just relayed what was taught to him with nothing of his own, according to Peter Yu, who's the founding director of an intellectual property program at the Michigan State University College of Law. Chinese lacked then a sense of individual rights anyway, so they would hardly think to *own* intellectual property. That's why copying another scholar's academic thesis into one's own needs no more of a citation than to write that the sun rises in the east. That said, I've found as a university instructor that most Gen X, Gen Z and Millennial students do use citations—just not for every passage that they copy.

Children today memorize poems and short stories in school. Many of their teachers ask students to learn vocabulary by copying definitions from dictionaries instead of coming up with their own based on a word's context in a longer passage. They're not normally asked to write their own. Copyrighted songs may be played at school ceremonies and chorus performances without consent from the relevant recording labels. I was miffed by these practices when my children went to grade school but remembered to insert myself into their cultural context instead of my own.

Those who copy and redistribute software or films aim to cheat, however, which is why they try to hide from inspectors. But most academics, authors and artists are just doing what's familiar.

One English major, for example, once proudly told me she had finished her senior thesis and asked whether I could review it as a native speaker. The then 23-year-old's English skills had soared above average, hence her pride. But she wasn't native, and I could tell that about half of her thesis was written in language typical of native speakers with a lot of letters behind their names. She had block copied those segments from textbooks and research papers without citations. When I asked why, she said that because she had not copied any author's entire text that the act didn't amount to plagiarism. Her grasp of plagiarism is typical among Chinese, likewise her benign yet nonchalant attitude.

Chinese laws, which have grown stricter under pressure from foreign governments and international trade associations, spell out clearly what's legal. But many copyright violations still lack the punitive responses that are often found in the West, and China in 2023 was facing a rash of patent hoarding to let copycats legalise their acts. Common people in China usually accept that they can copy and will be copied in the creative industries.

Now, China's feeling of competition with the West has re-legitimated copying without permission.

Chinese resented European and American forces for colonizing parts of the country that was already weak under the Qing Dynasty, so they adopted what Yu of Michigan State calls a 'self-strengthening worldview'. This view holds strong today despite China's economic growth and military prowess (with no further threat of colonialism) as Chinese leaders mould their population to think China should do better than other countries. Citizens further believe now it's "right to freely reproduce or to tolerate the unauthorized reproduction of foreign works that would help strengthen the country", Yu argues.

As China races the West for geopolitical clout, people's sense of competition has fostered a collective sense of copying for cause. The thinking is that widespread duplication of quality foreign software, films and product designs should help China leapfrog ahead without the labor and R&D that the West had invested to get wherever it is.

Copying, finally, just plain keeps common people safe. A century of turbulence, from the Nationalists' overthrow of the Qing Dynasty through the war with Japan and the Cultural Revolution, stoked fear in common people. The fearful survived that chaos by keeping quiet and neutral if not supportive of whoever appeared to be in power. They tried to blend safely with whatever force was sweeping the country. Copying was safe. Innovating raised doubts.

Today, duplication of creative works continues to deflect a different kind of suspicion, namely getting called out for errors, oversights and poor ideas in an office or classroom full of competitive rising stars. A content creator can say, "I got this from somewhere else, so don't blame me." This is hardly a China-only phenomenon.

Countless millions of Chinese people, of course, do original work.

China wouldn't have an Alibaba, a TikTok or a Tencent otherwise. But officials still let stores sell fake Apple gear and once even allowed a Starbucks lookalike café called "Starbuck" to operate across the street from the coastal city Qingdao's flagship tourist hotels. I went in myself for a coffee and, of course, to sleuth around for a news article on the innovative almost-violation of a trademark. The vendor was showing respect for a major brand while cutting the same brand down.

Almost is Good Enough

China is shrouded in imprecision. Instead of announcing that a project cost of 10.76 billion yuan, for example, a public construction agency in charge might say 'more than 10 billion yuan'. The agency's internal files show exact figures, but heavily rounded ones often pop out when secretive government offices must share the numbers publicly. We journalists encounter terms such as 'about, 'approximately' and 'more than' with a regularity that's aggravating when we're writing for foreign audiences who prefer precision. White lines on the streets advise against parking in bus stops, but plenty of cars cross the lines when convenient. A clerk's directions to the store given to a customer by phone might leave out a key cross street. If a store says on its website that it opens daily at 11 a.m., smart shoppers call first to make sure the gates don't swing open closer to 11:30 instead.

This historical habit of approximation thrives because vagueness keeps people safe. Imprecision protects oneself from harsh feedback and, more importantly, preserves relationships that exactitude could ruin.

As a newcomer to China and one used to more exactness, I first consulted research on Confucius, the Chinese philosopher of approximately 2,500 years ago. He described this approach to reality as the 'Doctrine of the Mean'. The doctrine says people should express tolerance toward one another if they're roughly in sync rather than imposing strict boundaries around their ideas, which could cause friction if one person's fact set differs from another's.

Chinese writer Hu Shi's essay 'Mr Chabuduo' reconfirms the prevalence of imprecision in a more sarcastic vein, I found after putting aside Confucius. (Cha bu duo is Mandarin for 'more or less'.) The protagonist in this work believes in approximation even after he misses a train by two minutes and ends up with the wrong doctor because he picked one with a surname almost but not exactly like the name of the doctor he wanted. At the end, he figures life and death are close enough, so why get too hung up chasing one over the other.

Precision is no stranger to China. Trains run ominously on time, something the US passenger rail system could learn from, and business meetings where both parties have something at stake start on schedule. The more publicity-conscious government agencies release needle-point figures nowadays to impress the world that they are careful and accurate. Yet both Hu Shi and Confucius remain highly relevant today.

Compliance with the Doctrine of the Mean keeps harmony by averting disputes that could arise from insistence on exact results. Disputes can get extra ugly in China because the country lacks a fair, steadfast system for legal arbitration. The lack of exact terms allows for wiggle room, a safe way to say "that's not what I meant," if challenged. Vagueness lets relationships flourish, say between two potential business partners, by delaying the most likely source of disagreement—precise terms. A final, detailed transaction can be worked out when personal relations are solid.

Strong relations are paramount for getting ahead in Chinese

society. Success in work and wealth accumulation hinges largely on personal connections. Social, political and economic chaos going back hundreds of years have challenged trust among strangers, so deep connections weigh heavier in China than they might in a more stable society. Stronger legal systems and social welfare in Western countries protect transactions, creations and investments. Chinese governments from dynastic times onward have tilted their energy more toward major affairs of state than protecting common people.

There's a flip side, of course, as I discovered from the literature: "cha bu duo," British writer and China hand James Palmer writes in a 2016 online essay, is "a phrase you'll hear with grating regularity, one that speaks to a job seventy percent done, a plan sketched out but never completed, a gauge unchecked, or a socket put in the wrong size". This type of corner-cutting abounds in China, and vagueness about one's work offers a defense for the lazy.

I once traveled from my base in Beijing to the city of Qiqihar in northeastern China to interview senior people at a university for a news feature about training students to teach the purest spoken Mandarin in a vast country foaming with mutually unintelligible dialects. The city's foreign affairs office set up the interviews and my schedule. It turned out that Qiqihar doesn't really have China's cleanest Mandarin. That honor probably belongs to a city such as Shijiazhuang or Shenzhen where migrants from around the country become dominant enough to reduce the influence of local dialects. The university was training teachers based largely on a *belief* that Qiqihar was the fountainhead of pure Mandarin—a belief that I had shared based on the widespread views of my Chinese friends. The university felt it had given me an almost-is-good-enough account of what I was after, basically a few figures about how well their teachers could, or should, advance Mandarin purity around the country. I went on to write a 'cha bu duo' report based on the figures provided and a few interviews.

The trip was mostly about bonding. The city and the school promoted themselves to a foreign journalist who was keen to cover a quirk of China's culture and education rather than write another scathing political piece. If I ever needed something again from Qiqihar, the foreign affairs office would oblige. That help would go a long way if a natural disaster struck, for instance, and the media need official information quickly. (I've yet to cash in.)

China's deals with historically distrusted countries start out too with vague wording that builds bilateral relations, because officials want to know the other government means well before plunging into the gutsier, we-shall details. Chinese leaders feel safest when nothing is being given away and hope the upbeat language softens the other party.

When Beijing signed an Economic Cooperation Framework Agreement with Taipei in 2010, the two sides lowered tariffs for just 800 import categories, leaving thousands more up for later negotiation. The agreement's seven pages draw heavily on feel-good phrases such as 'strengthen cross-Strait economic exchange and cooperation', a reference to the ocean strait between them. The Mainland Chinese side veered away from substantive action in order to establish harmony with Taiwan, a political rival since the 1940s. Relations have plummeted since 2016, and as of 2023 the two sides had never touched the remaining import categories. In 2023, mainland officials in fact scaled back the 2010 agreement

To smooth things over with the Philippines in 2016 after it had won World Court (The International Court of Justice) arbitration over a maritime sovereignty dispute, China pledged $24 billion in investment and aid but without specific projects or exact timelines. China can release that money over any period it wants. Chinese leaders further pledged to explore for offshore oil and gas with the Philippines in the South China Sea, the site of their sovereignty dispute, but without specific proposals. The two sides went back to bickering in 2018 and have slung mud well into 2023. Filipino scholars whom I've interviewed say most of the pledged money never made it and the two countries have yet to cooperate on fossil fuels. China's lack of specific promises gave it the safety offered by the Doctrine of the Mean.

What's Up with Gambling, from Macau to the Financial Markets?

It's a smart bet China and gambling have some kind of synergy. Before Covid-19 choked off most inbound travel, Macau reigned as the world's biggest casino city by revenue because of its ties with China. China administers the former Portuguese colony and most of casino customers come from China. Macau's casinos need not rely on Las Vegas-style gimmicks such as ultra-cheap meals and children's play areas to tempt customers. Macau is as expensive as Hong Kong, and that's saying a lot. Casino security people dressed like Men in Black bounce customers who deign, as I once did, to wear shorts or, as I also once did, display their own deck of cards in a lobby restaurant. Chinese normally stream through the territory's tiny single-terminal airport year-round to reach giant compounds such as the Venetian and the Parisian because they're consumed by gambling. Macau is just the most ostentatious example. Stock traders often buy and sell with a gambler's mindset. Property speculators think the same way, as do poker players at family parties.

Gambling, if done professionally to play up strategy over luck, represents the fastest route to wealth in a country where common sources of income are considered insecure or just not fast enough. That's why so many people get into it.

Quick money raises one's confidence and financial fitness in a chaotic country where assets can be taken away due to bouts of socio-political upheaval and weak legal protection—topics covered in chapters 26 and 30. China was mostly poor until the 1980s. Not so many decades ago, most people farmed, fished, mined, toiled in factories or worked in some supporting role. Others drove heavy trucks on dangerous highways. They didn't all make enough money to afford comfortable housing and full medical treatment. They might have died instead before their fifties due to years of toiling without steady healthcare. Chinese families as far away from China as San Francisco have told me these stories.

But China sat at the end of enough cross-border trading routes over the centuries for citizens to realize they could make money without ploughs, trucks and gruelling labor. As trade flourished, so did intermediaries—the people who make money from being in the right places at the right times to facilitate trade, rather than from producing actual goods. Intermediaries fostered a psychology of earning money without intense labor, and sometimes with quick turnover. Bettors do the same thing, just better.

Back to the baccarat tables, I confess to suck at gambling, so I checked for other sources and found a revealing 2018 *Yale Tribune* study of studies. It says Chinese as well as other Asians take to gambling partly because of beliefs in superstition and luck. And a disproportionate number of addicted gamblers afflict Asian populations in the United States compared to the general population because of this faith in luck, fortune and fate, according to a 2014 article on the medical news website *Psychology Today*. I know of a billboard in the San Francisco Bay

Area advertising help for gambling addiction. The billboard model is a penitent-looking Asian man.

But luck and superstition don't penetrate the hardcore gambler's psychology. These beliefs mainly just get gamblers to try casinos occasionally to see how it goes. More experienced gamblers, the ones on a fast-money track, believe a pro can devise ways to make money from a casino despite statistical odds favoring the house. Customers in Macau casinos have gone from table to table playing baccarat in 'stealth mode', for example, according to one study. Other players have plotted together at a single table against the house even if they are technically adversaries among themselves. Theoretically, if the group collusion works, they all win at least a small amount. Some players chat up dealers to tease out information before a round. These schemes take skill that not everyone has.

Casinos are banned in Mainland China and not everyone can afford travel to Macau whenever the gambling urge strikes. Perhaps most people in China are thrifty, wise and income-confident enough to spurn gambling for their whole lives anyway. Most Chinese people whom I've met describe themselves with those adjectives but know of a friend or relative who gambles — without ever visiting a casino. To serve those bettors, so many informal, illegal gambling schemes permeate China outside of Macau that the laws against them only take up space on paper.

The schemes start in homes where families play mahjong, poker, blackjack and dice games during holidays. Siblings and cousins might bet against one another for money with the same intensity of someone sweating over a final exam. Men in some cities play home-cooked betting games with the same fervor in outdoor cafes. Online sports betting is rampant. I walked into a 2022 Christmas party in Hong Kong where several couples and their grown children were yelling and hooting as they placed bets—and took one another's own money.

A final exam taker's level of intensity at a game such as poker means money wasn't put down just for fun, nor does anyone expect a boost from pure fortune as in horoscopic alignments. These players clearly fancy themselves professionals like those who believe enough skill can outsmart a casino.

Property speculators typically think the same way. Whether in China or in a major foreign city, Chinese owners of houses and apartments can be found talking the roof off about 'flipping' properties. I've sat through several discussions with Chinese immigrants in the San Francisco Bay Area about who's got the most flippable properties or made the most money from a flip. Property is the all-time safest type of investment, per the usual thinking in China, since it offers something real, immediate and unlikely to go away. The gambling mindset leads many real estate investors to leverage debt so they can buy up multiple properties and sell as soon as the market price rises. Flipping is a strategic risk-and-return mindset like the one found among players in the Macau casinos. Mastery takes brain sweat.

The same approach applies to capital markets. About 148 million personal investors, the biggest population in any single country, invest in Chinese stocks, according to my employer, the Hong Kong media outlet the *South China Morning Post*. Most are Chinese nationals. Many expect quick returns from a gain in share prices rather than a long hold-and-see period of the type that experienced financial advisers recommend. This approach has been blamed for the crazy ups and downs on Chinese stock exchanges since 2015, according to the people I've interviewed for news stories about the markets. The Chinese markets fell hard in 2015 partly because brokers had convinced mom-and-pop traders to take out loans for initial investments and later try short-selling, which means betting on a stock's early demise.

That's a big gamble and not one for the casual luck-and-fortune follower.

Trucking, welding and factory work today pay enough to afford a passable life for the immediate family. These occupations require no gamble and little of the harrowing intensity that permeates betting for quick money. One's income won't bobble up and down like a yacht in a squall. Yet the *People's Daily* newspaper once estimated that China had 88 vacancies for every experienced, skilled blue-collar worker and 16 vacancies for every factory technician, my ongoing research found. And this scarcity had slowed production in China even pre-pandemic, recruitment consultancy ManpowerGroup's China office once said.

These jobs simply don't vault anyone ahead like the right play in property, stocks and baccarat.

Never Pay Full Price—There's Always Another Way

In China, the posted prices on a lot of merchandise serve only as a vague idea of what a consumer must actually pay. Most experienced sellers expect to haggle. Prices come down if shoppers buy two or three of something. Rewards-point programs abound. Some stores drop prices for students, the elderly, workers in certain companies and bearers of hard-to-get coupons. Smart shoppers often start an adventure by canvassing relatives and friends about whether they know of any technically available discounts that merchants don't mention on their own. Consumers seldom expect to pay full posted prices, except for the most sundry of stuff such as food and stationery—and vendors in the fruit market nearest my flat in Beijing were even opening to haggling over a kilo of oranges.

These elaborate quests to drive down prices thrive in China despite rapid gains in household wealth, because memories of poverty sustain latent fears of not having enough money for basic needs, a huge incentive to shop for the best prices at whatever effort. Another factor: Chinese society operates more on relationships of convenience than by set rules. An immutable price tag represents a rule. Just about everyone knows sellers will take the best price they believe they can get. Getting the truly lowest price requires bargaining a seller down to that bottom line.

Foreigners, if new to China, may assume posted prices are the only prices if that's how commerce works in their homelands. It took me the first couple of years in Beijing to look past those prices. I was used to moderate household income and fixed price-setting rules in my US homeland. Those of us fresh off the plane might lack access to local people who could tell us how to get discounts. (The once common, officially sanctioned, higher-than-market-rate 'foreigner prices' in China has gone virtually extinct.)

First sign the specter of poverty is talking: shoppers gather more thickly at outdoor produce markets, also called 'wet' markets, than at supermarkets in much of China because the prices are lower. Vendors pay less in overhead for a market stall than for a clean, lighted, air-conditioned indoor store, and their savings get passed on to shoppers. Consumers worried about money — for real or due to fear of not having enough someday — shop the wet markets even though some of the older ones are sweaty, dark, far from home and possibly full of rats.

Price-wary shoppers of more expensive goods, such as home appliances and flashy clothing, may grill vendors about the big-name brands but often can't drive the price down as far as the off-brand lookalikes. Lookalikes offer the same status as a branded product among one's many peers who believe the imitation to be real. But most off-brand phones, jackets and shoes fall apart within months of a purchase, I found over my years in Beijing. No small number of Chinese consumers use inexpensive non-Apple handsets shaped like the original for $290 instead of $990.

Historic poverty across so many generations extends this

cost-conscious mindset to much of the global Chinese diaspora, even its wealthiest people. Despite owning a $2 million mansion in the hills above Stanford University, for example, a Chinese family out at the mall might draw more on the frugal teachings of their elders than the less thrifty American consumer culture that surrounds them. That said, consumer diversity is as strong among Chinese as any other group. Particularly in lookalike iPhones, for example, cheaper phones might freeze every day and must be switched off and restarted for normal functioning. The average price-wary phone owner just puts up with this technical problem, among others. Friends still enviously gawk because they fancy the phone holder as a person of status, so it was worth paying the equivalent of $290. In some families with a long trans-generational history of wealth, Chinese spend as wildly as American youth portrayed in Hollywood dramas. Gift shopping is particularly writ large.

Whether in a lower middle-class district of China or in a swanky majority-Chinese neighborhood in California, conversation at family gatherings may drill down into how one among them can shave a few dollars off an upcoming purchase. The exchanges usually start with an unwitting sacrificial story-sharer who says, "Guess what everyone, I paid just 50 RMB for a sweatshirt down at the department store because they're having a sale." This narrator hopes for a 'what a great deal' reply but usually sees a group of gaping mouths and saucer eyes. One of the gapers might say, 'So expensive!? I know someone who got that sweatshirt at the outdoor clothing alley for just 30 RMB." Another will talk about a friend who got it for 20 RMB. Eventually they'll all agree about where the best deals are so the original storyteller can be more careful next time and any other shoppers can take note. My tip, from experience: don't tell people what you pay for stuff unless you want a backlash.

In China, aversion to rules in favor of relationships (see Chapter 31) offers further reason to haggle for lower prices. Disrespect for rules hardly stops or ends at price setting. Cars regularly drive on China's sidewalks and food stands pop up in places where the signage says don't. The Chinese government has taken control over much of the disputed South China Sea, even sailing into the UN-proscribed exclusive economic zones of other countries. It knows the UN boundaries mean less to Brunei, Malaysia and the Philippines than the aid, trade and investment that China offers them in exchange for ignoring the UN formula.

Price-setting exchanges between shoppers and sellers have become a sport in China. I learned this exchange through practice, timid and awkward at first, then more officious little by little until it became habit. The usual exchange goes like this: the shopper asks first whether posted prices reflect the biggest possible discount. If the answer is yes, persistent shoppers should ask how the same item sells for less somewhere else, possibly a lie. The vendor replies with an offer between the posted price and the elsewhere price. The shopper walks away. The vendor says come back. Chatter about any coupons, senior discounts, rewards programs cross the table at this point. The players eventually reach a deal. Tourists can find this style of bargaining in Beijing taken to extremes at a clothing and foreigner-focused souvenir market called Silk Alley. Foreigners like the former me may recoil at first but ease into the game once they realize merchants don't mind bargaining, evidenced by the calm shopkeeper smile that says, "I've had this kind of chat a thousand times."

Consumers from well-off Western countries may still see talking down the price on something simple such as a T-shirt as just a ritual for ritual's sake. They probably lack a shared memory of living on dangerously low incomes. China has that collective recall, and it drives searches in China for the absolute lowest prices. Shoppers from outside China may be used to following fixed rules, too, rather than plumbing each vendor's bottom line.

The Customer Is Always Right, as Long as the Company Agrees

Disputes between merchants and customers can get heated fast over paltry refund requests. In other cases around China, customers might say a device they bought broke on its own and the vendor accuses the customer of breaking it, sparking a warranty dispute. I had this blow-up with a landlady when her fridge started making jet engine noises one day. A plane ticket might show the wrong date. A call never made pops up on a phone bill. At an upmarket restaurant in Beijing, a man with a cheap black nylon jacket sits down with a couple of sparkly liquor bottles and two women no more than two-thirds his age, plus a few of his business associates. His party gets served ahead of a customer who had ordered earlier, because of his apparent status or familiarity with the restaurant operator. I've been that customer who came in first. And when service is slow bordering on none, I've asked waiters to cancel orders. I'm usually told, "Your food is already prepared and will be out in a flash." It's easily a lie, but the restaurant doesn't want anyone to leave without paying. A customer who takes off anyway risks an argument with the restaurant managers.

These cases show the customer isn't always so right in China, and three reasons explain why. First, there's a broad belief the house has more status than the guest. Second, less experienced or more old-fashioned businesspeople think short term about income and fret more about losing money in today's one-off dispute than about retaining a customer's future business by settling the one-off at a small loss. Finally, China lacks a reliable, pro-consumer complaint system to help settle disputes.

The axiom, "the customer is always right," coined in 1909 by the founder of a London department store, permeates service culture in much of the West. In China too, most retailers don't fib, cheat, sacrifice quality, decline refunds or change an order without notice—the usual problems whenever problems come up. The economy wouldn't perform otherwise. But a noticeable number of merchants in China still don't buy the customer-service axiom.

A seller's status as the 'house' is supposed to give it the upper hand over consumers. Vendors who believe this status equation figure they're bigger than their customers because they have more assets than a mere individual. They have building space, a brand, a staff and a set of uniforms, for example. Plenty of common people, by the same token, aspire to the status of business owner. They follow a Confucian reverence for the powerful and have a practical sense that anything with scale must be doing more things better than those without it (otherwise how would they have achieved scale?). Many in China even pay higher prices than in other countries for status merchandise such as watches and wines so they can experience that status.

The notion of classless Marxism-Leninism held mass appeal mainly in the 1950s after the communist government had taken power based on that doctrine. Wealthier now, a lot of Chinese have gone back to an earlier comfort zone of assigning class according to perceived worth. Whether now or centuries ago, ordering fellow humans by their worth in one's mind can help people size up an often opaque, unregulated society and to know their place in it.

According to this order, enterprises as small as a one-room neighborhood clothing store have higher status than the common shopper. The store at least has a parcel of land and a physical enclosure. Bigger outlets claim all that plus piles of paperwork to prove who they are along with lists of rules that they flash during disputes even if they don't apply to a customer's specific request. That documentation boosts legitimacy as most of their customers can't normally muster any competing sheaf of paperwork during disputes.

Chinese merchants too often think short term because in big chunks of history only that outlook made sense. War, famine and other sudden changes have dominated the centuries, so why get hung up on a ten-year business growth map? A hit-or-miss legal system in China means a local official can technically come along and demand a cut of some merchant's revenue, perhaps claiming the store didn't follow building codes even if similar stores hardly ever follow the codes. Natural disasters periodically wipe out family farms. Farmers just start over the next season after borrowing money from family to get by until then. Vendors for this reason easily panic at the idea of losing a sale today. They're not conditioned to consider instead the long-term impact of losing a customer who, if happy now, could spend hundreds of times the disputed amount in future business.

Diners and shoppers encounter service staffers more often than they see managers. Staff people tend to stand their ground viciously in customer disputes to avoid any blame for lost business. A few quickly apologize to make problems go away. Usually they pull rank, house over guest. For example, when negotiating what to do about a botched product repair, shops almost always ask customers to return to the counter on their own time and expense, rather than sending a representative out to meet the customer. In my experience, only the threat of calling out an irresponsible vendor on social media gets the management's attention.

Consumers have no reliable protection from on high, in turn giving businesspeople confidence to pull rank over customers. Anyone can freely call the 12315 complaint hotline or use 12315.cn to report problems with merchants. The average jilted consumer hardly ever uses the service, for lack of faith that it will help. I've never tried it either, believing as locals do that it's not useful, so I did a bit of research. I found a passage in the *Chinese Journal of Comparative Law,* arguing Chinese courts strive for a 'delicate balance' between encouraging consumers to "pursue fraudulent traders" while "discouraging consumers from exploiting the punitive damages provisions of the Consumer Protection Law".

People in China generally know all this either from experience or intuitively, so they smarten up before going out. They know restaurant wait people could say an order is almost ready even when the cooks haven't started making the first dish and that merchants might claim customers caused whatever product defects they report. Perhaps they have called their property owners about broken air-con and been told: "that never happened when the last tenant lived there." Wily consumers rightly suspect too those bigger institutions can unfurl fancy lists of printed, chop-stamped rules to justify a surcharge the customer never heard about before—possibly because it was never there before.

These savvy shoppers reduce their risk by consulting friends about honest merchants and compare notes to avoid businesses with a record of scams. My wife and I have tapped friends over the years to recommend air-con vendors, dentists, travel agents, plumbers and electricians to avoid the dangers of picking random people from an internet search. Dishonest vendors who keep at it long enough do lose business, but new ones will keep popping up to challenge consumers on their repairs, refunds, warranties and wait times before meals.

Part IV
Chinese Society and the World

Curiosity and How it Helps

Chinese people typically shower friends and strangers alike with questions. Foreigners in China should expect to be asked to disclose their salaries and describe living conditions in their homelands. I lost count of how many Beijing taxi drivers asked me about both within a minute after I had hopped in and closed the door. At dinner parties, four or five young people might spray questions for half an hour at a PhD student acquaintance about what it's like in graduate school, a pursuit shrouded in mystique among common people. Dinner party goers would ask any editors at the table about whether her or his news organization has ever killed a story before press time because of political sensitivities. One who has recently bought property would anticipate getting grilled on the price, the quality and whether the developer delivered on promises such as insulating the water pipes. Someone like me who rents in the expensive inner cities gets a derivative of that question: how much do you pay per month?

The urge to learn about other people is indisputably human. It's on Maslow's hierarchy of human needs. But Chinese seek information through personal contacts with a uniquely intense zeal. Why do they do it, why so often, why so many questions and why not get the information some other way? The keenness for questions requites a crush to keep up with a vast, fast-changing but opaque country including its hit-or-miss relations with rest of the world. I learned that when asking people why they were asking questions.

The government carefully controls information released online, through the mass media and in school textbooks. The police and China's chief online messaging service WeChat help check published, posted content for anything that they think threatens the state or social stability. Censorship penetrates everyday interaction despite China's overall population size, to wit: erased WeChat dialogues among friends who touch on a sensitive topic.

But information is like a virus. It finds a way past secured barriers. That's because shared individual experiences usually leave stronger impressions than material in books, mass media and websites. By example, a fruitful year of study abroad could temper one's notions about China being inherently, vastly superior to other countries. Students I know have told me as much. Losing in court to a developer over failure to disclose structural problems in a new flat suggests China isn't always ruled by law, as it claims. People with these experiences tell others when asked.

It's particularly tough for non-traveling locals to grasp what's happening outside China. Travel costs money and time. There can be tough immigration barriers. Mass media promote a unique version of life overseas—replete with demons (US officials) and heroes (China's leadership). For this reason, people generally see China as a benevolent yet historically oppressed country whose time has come to get its just deserts, be that a pro-Beijing trade deal with another country or rights to the East China Sea, despite competing claims from Japan (another media demon). Domestic media and required school textbooks turn up with quotes about Westerners being lazy and cold yet somehow wealthy. Countries poorer than China get relatively little media attention unless the Chinese government is propping them up economically or they're in a dispute with Beijing.

Yet the information in domestic news reports about Sino-foreign relations meets with considerable suspicion among the Chinese who intuitively know nothing in life is a simple as hero-versus-demon. Meeting foreigners gives those doubtful citizens chances to fact-check. Answers from the foreigner will contribute information, even if just a smidgeon, to the growing Chinese reservoir of uncensored knowledge. Answer-seekers do not necessarily act on new information. They're more likely to use answers to color in the grey areas on their overall impressions of the world. For that reason, even if I tired of questions or found them remotely offensive, I calmly answered almost all of them.

Expatriates in China can add much to that reservoir by disclosing rent they pay in China versus overseas, the value of wages and property at home and the prices they pay while in China (the same as everyone else). Many ask foreigners too for confirmation of widely reported news events. They will query for example the American race-related riots of 2020, which Chinese media jumped on—a way to discredit another big country and make their own look clean by comparison. Sino-foreign political disputes generate plenty of questions from curious commoners. Deeper discussions might test common stereotypes. Are the French really a romantic people, a Chinese news reader have asked visitors. Some Chinese school textbooks say Americans have distant relations with family members and a chronically lazy way of living, though blessed with wealth simply by living in the United States. Americans in China have a chance to share their own views. I've shared plenty of mine.

Common people can freely express themselves in private voice-to-voice situations. If polite, even spreaders of contrarian views get taken seriously with little risk of losing friends. Questions are normally phrased politely, too. The askers usually realize that conventional ideas, such everyone in a giant country being romantic or lazy, are as empirically impossible as hero-versus-demon scenarios. Author Arthur Smith's book *Chinese Characteristics* notes a politeness, benevolence and fear of offending other people as national traits. I was encouraged to read it. Those traits prime many people to ask questions that show respect.

A Beijing taxi driver circa 2000 once asked me about my wife, who was born in China. The driver was particularly interested in our ages, which are two years apart. My answer satisfied the driver because he had imagined Western men preferred significantly younger Chinese women. His view changed on the spot. Had he not asked, the suspicion that all foreign men marry women ten years their junior would have persisted.

The Chinese quiz one another even more rigorously than they test foreigners. Close friends, trusted coworkers, and university classmates make ideal Q&A subjects. Strangers need a bit of feeling out. One stranger will bristle at questions, while the next one will take them in stride and like the attention. Local-to-local question sessions have yielded answers about where the latest SARS cluster might be, going back to 2003. They ferret out information about what structures will fall next in a neighborhood slated for redevelopment and when new projects will be done. Official health updates and redevelopment are notoriously opaque in China. And as Chapter 33 explains, there's endless querying on what others have paid for goods and services.

In another case, I once filed a police report about a year's worth of daily text messages aimed at swaying my news coverage to be more anti-government. I had asked the anonymous sender to quit, but he found ways to keep harassing me. My company didn't have any other mobile numbers to assign. The case officer in Beijing asked enough questions to fill two sheets of a yellow legal pad. At the end he told me he couldn't help. The officer's keen notetaking showed more of an urge to explore a little known element of his society than to crack a case, I later reflected.

When a Smiling Face Is Hiding Hostility

Sometimes everyone looks so happy it's hard to imagine any discord in China. Expatriates who work in an office of mostly Chinese colleagues may meet with immediate verbal approval from colleagues for their every idea, from let's grab lunch to let's start a management revolution, along with fawning praise for completion of small tasks such as proofreading a hundred words of non-native English. When I was new to the country and clueless about how to read faces, I misread lots of *China Daily* colleagues as awestruck by my willingness to help with their English. In truth, the Chinese colleagues could find a foreigner to be a pain at the office and I know a couple people felt that about me for a while. In the same spirit, teachers in China may be told they're the best the school ever had — by students who feel baffled by their lectures. When shoppers spill sacks of food on crowded sidewalks, they often look back at the gawkers, but they wear victory smiles. When I saw a woman do this in Beijing, I started to suspect something was up. Could she really be happy?

False smiles and affirmative reactions to negative stimuli —

especially to fear and anger—pervade human interaction in China. People can be direct as well, given their country's massive diversity across a 1.4 billion population. But the prevailing trend is to mask ill sentiments. The smiles and yesses reflect a broad desire to get along, especially with opaque yet potentially powerful individuals, such as teachers, in a society that runs more on relationships than rules.

Political scientists believe the powerless and the uninformed worldwide act to please others out of fear. They're afraid a verbal or nonverbal 'no' would spark retaliation, one of my university professors said. To quote an old metaphor, smiling yes-people give 'face' to the feared, the influential and the unknown. The receivers of brilliant smiles and personal compliments are supposed to feel so good that they won't suspect that the face-givers might have a disagreement. The award of face sustains relations with co-workers, salvages disputes with merchants and pleases superiors in China. It's hard to know when someone might need favors from these people.

Chinese colleagues who flatter foreigners in the office are probably trying to get along with an unknown yet possibly influential entity. Most Chinese lack a deep understanding of foreigners, due to little exposure over their lifetimes. A foreigner in the office might do something quirky under pressure, the fear goes. We Westerners on the *China Daily* copy desk would talk louder and express bolder opinions to one another compared to our Chinese colleagues. Naturally no one wants to be around when some quirk suddenly explodes. Entrepreneurs, government office clerks, workplace supervisors and even strangers with unclear intentions often get the same yes-yes-yes treatment. They all have a measure of power that could be wielded without warning.

Teachers have obvious influence over grades and

recommendations, perhaps the reason for this case: a university student in Beijing once asked me, her instructor of six months, for a graduate school recommendation letter. She was scoring around 70 in the class but showed an ambitious spirit that had already landed her a job with China Central Television. She fawned with thanks at the composite score of 80 on my recommendation letter. The student had angrily shredded the letter because she expected a higher score, I found out from one of her classmates. Months later, she asked me to appear on one of her TV shows when she suddenly needed guests. By thanking me for the score of 80, the student had saved relations despite her anger.

Lots of smiles and praise are genuine. An expression of thanks to a foreign colleague who volunteers ten minutes to proofread someone's English should be a real one. It would be anywhere. But if the thanks veer into comments about how the foreigner is a language superstar and gift to the Chinese people, someone's probably exaggerating. Thanks that follow a list of specific reasons, such as the grateful individual gaining knowledge of specific English vocabulary and points of grammar, should mean the person really feels warm about the encounter. Someone who doesn't even look over the translation but praises it effusively may just want the good-relations door left open in case he needs more help later, a tribute to the foreigner's influence as a fluent speaker of English.

Asking a colleague to lunch gets murkier. The initial smile-and-thanks of acceptance augur well. But the invitee might privately worry after a bit more thought about who will pay, whether uncomfortable issues will loom over the cashew chicken and what other colleagues will think. The invitee could back out with an easy excuse about being busy or sick once the dining time gets closer.

A winner's smile and bow of thanks in response to criticism from a workplace superior — as if to say it's purely constructive — would seldom be genuine. The superior helped build the workplace. It's her or his baby. Any positive feedback would be aimed at making a potentially angry, irascible critic go away without a scene. As one example, ten of us Western copy editors at *China Daily* had once been grumbling to the head copy editor, a Chinese national and our direct supervisor, about hidden advertising and not-so-hidden pro-China political statements in the international news. One day, that supervisor organized a half-day outing to the Summer Palace, a Beijing historical landmark. *China Daily* hired a bus and paid for everyone's lunch. When I asked whether I was supposed to talk about the advertising and propaganda on that outing, the supervisor said he had been waiting for me to raise the issues. The trip had all but ended at that point, and the topic never came up again.

Genuine pleasure in China looks a lot like it does in other places: wide, relaxed, sustained smiles from the mouth into the eyes, with more than just a quick burst of laughter. A smile that hides anger, fear, grief or confusion shows a lot of facial muscle and fades fast. The eyes don't smile. Compliments are stiff and awkward, even if effusive. This kind of reaction manifests when someone spills a sack full of belongings in a crowd. The grinning face tells bystanders, 'I'm fine despite the mishap'.

Chinese people typically see overt expressions of anger, grief and despair as personal weaknesses. Those expressions suggest that someone can't handle ordinary daily setbacks such as dropping their stuff. Employers, colleagues and potential spouses are looking instead for Teflon teammates in a country where ongoing developmental issues can make life pretty tough. Smiling from the ground, surrounded by spilt oranges and bags of fish, tells bystanders that setbacks are simple and conquerable.

Here's a tale that tells all. There was once a Beijing television program presenter who asked me to join her on a talk show requiring Chinese-language skills. The program's recruiter was looking specifically for a foreigner. I had lived in Beijing just a few months and my Chinese sucked. She asked me as well to refer a foreign-born friend for the same program so she would have two guests. I found a British colleague to help and his Chinese sucked too. The recruiter eventually found more qualified people and ditched both of us by avoiding my calls. But our channel of communication never technically closed, so if the program needed us in the future, she could reach out again. She knew her country operated on relationships.

Why You Get Someone to Guide You Everywhere

Getting directions in China can be as murky as a navigating a maze in the haze. Instead of being told how many blocks to walk and what landmarks to look for—let alone compass points—people asking how to get places may be urged to go 'down that way' or 'over there' with hand motions for emphasis. I lost hours of valuable time following these directions before online maps became the norm. After I went down that way or over there, as instructed, I would usually need to ask at least one other person what to do. Oddly, the street-side savants giving directions know exactly where these places are. They're just not used to explaining.

In China, people commonly go to new places with human guides rather than maps. After a couple of trips to some place with a friend or relative who's gone before, these commuters, shoppers, drivers and tourists remember the route without checking street signs.

The reliance on guides rests at the intersection of two Chinese states of mind: a vague suspicion of the unknown and a belief that a trusted, experienced person can most safely navigate the unknown. A sense of hospitality toward outsiders, especially those who are lost, makes guides readily available.

Unknown grids of streets would daunt just about anyone who's pressed for time or dependent on complex mass transit networks, both of which are norms in urban China. Mobile phones come with real-time locator maps, and people who grow up on the technology use them liberally. But anxiety about striking out alone was around before today's urbanization. Centuries of hand-me-down fears about the unknown still steer a lot of citizens to use human guides.

Nothing has ever been 100 percent precise in China, even if a map says so. Once upon a time, one who made a wrong turn would step into a river or onto a property claimed by a rival clan. Today a wrong turn easily exposes the wayward traveler to groups of gawking strangers, an off-limits military base or a row of Beijing shops where people sell drugs. I've been shooed away from PLA housing. I've walked into hotels dripping with prostitutes. More often, I turn some corner to find pods of men who've never seen a foreigner and won't take their eyes off me. On the other side of China's wealth divide, a lost middle-class commuter might stray into a luxurious neighborhood, the type of place where the denizens got rich on graft money and resent strangers for ogling their assets.

Intercity travelers normally expect friends and family at the destination to guide them for free. The hosts oblige because of their good relations, of course, but also because of pride, the idea that locals *should* take visitors under their care. Locals all but compulsively tell family, friends and even new acquaintances, "When you come to my hometown, I'll be your guide." Is someone already on the way? The local-slash-host should call ahead to find a hotel, make time to show off local tourist attractions and treat the visitor to at least one meal a day. Sometimes they offer pickups and drop-offs at railway stations.

A transplant who spends long enough in a new city becomes a guide for people back home. He could be a twenty-year-old who moves from the countryside to Beijing for university studies. She or he might be an entrepreneur who moves from a town along the Yangtze to Guangzhou to build their business. Cousins, aunts, uncles, old friends and new friends can tap these transplants as guides when they're visiting the person's adopted city. The most observant ones drop everything to be a guide-slash-host, even if they must cancel work and study. Guests more often than not politely reply, "No worries, we'll figure things out by ourselves," but everyone knows they're supposed to enjoy the transplant's hospitality, and the transplant usually obliges.

On my way one freezing day from Beijing to Baotou for two days for research, I ran into a university student on the train. She was a Baotou native and spent six hours over the coming day showing me an urban wild deer park and the city's signature steel factories. She felt obligated because she had grown up there. In another case, a university student once took me on a 45-minute city bus ride from the Wuhan main railway station to the humongous city's lake district. He had overheard me asking someone else for directions and understood his culturally prescribed role as a local guide for someone unfamiliar with his city.

Today's guides hardly ever fear the guest will encounter druggies, soldiers and super-rich weirdoes, much less an overflowing river or a hostile next-door village. They have simply seen their elders treat visitors the same way. They imitate elders.

Known, friendly people best qualify as guides, because the real game is about easing a newcomer's suspicion about a strange place. When groups of Chinese, especially elders, travel overseas, most of them hire tour guides rather than go solo backpacking. Guides meet the tourists at the airport, arrange all local transport and pick hotels. They jump off the bus with the tourists to describe attractions. Preferred guides are fellow Chinese people based in the destination countries. These guides erase any anxiety about going before a hotel counter oneself to negotiate rates and figure out a local bus system in a foreign language. There's a common language. There's a familiar face in an unknown land, which is the eeriest of unmarked intersections.

Even years after immigration to another country, Chinese may hang together for business, education and socializing, rather than getting to know dominant races in their new homelands.

Back to asking for street directions, a local who says, "I don't know quite how to tell you," or something else close to the truth would come off as a poor host for letting the stranger waste time fumbling around on his own. For this reason, most locals do their best. They gesticulate and say, "Over there, down that way". These replies might not help a lost pedestrian, but they make the local feel that hospitality has been extended.

When to Donate to Charity

It might appear that Chinese people don't give much to charitable causes — until suddenly they go mad for one. Middle-class Beijing people whom I've known write off beggars on the streets outside the diplomatic compounds as closet princes who got rich panhandling to foreigners. It's considered risky to help people lying in the street, injured by a car accident, even if every objective sign says they need help. A helper might be dragged into the police case or blamed for the accident. But then something comes up and tugs at everyone's conscience. The 2008 Sichuan earthquake that killed 70,000 people was one of those. Within the first 20 days after the quake, Chinese had given 42.74 billion yuan in relief money, plus more in material donations, through local governments and large-scale domestic charities such as the Red Cross Society of China.

When to donate comes down partly to individual taste and Chinese aren't the only people in the world who keep a bit of charity in their own pockets. But Chinese hold the donation bar higher than citizens would in some other countries because their own incomes still feel shaky despite a few decades of quick advances. And due to China's abundance of scams, people worry donation seekers don't need money at all (the Beijing beggars) or those who do need help (an accident victim) but could exploit their situation to seek more aid than required for recuperation. Donations come more willingly when a trusted person or institution is collecting the money.

The personal income concern reflects China's recent modernization coupled with lingering uncertainty about where the economy is headed. Middle-class Chinese represented just 3.1 percent of the population in 2000, and in 2018 it was more than half, or 707 million people, the Center for Strategic & International Studies think tank estimates. But people older than age fifty easily remember times before the 1980s when they lived more poorly and how hard it was to get ahead. The economy, despite its headline growth figures over the past twenty years, still undergoes assaults such as the 2015 stock market fall and the widespread lockdowns to control coronavirus infections in 2020 and 2022. Those downswings scare not a few people into thinking China's broader economic advances remain fragile.

Fear of false representation has plenty of grounding, too. Few beggars are outright rich or even middle class, but some have made a comfortable career of hustling money from strangers on the street—even hiring gangs of children to do it—because begging in a high-income part of town can pay more and faster than more orthodox work does. My Chinese friends in Beijing divulged all these suspicions when I asked, or when we were walking outside, and a child beggar started tugging at our trousers.

A man lying in the street after, say, a bike wreck does need help but may exploit a generous bystander by asking for more money than needed or falsely accusing the helper of causing the accident to demand a payout if police get involved. One friend, a middle-aged Chinese man, said he had once tried to help a stranger carry her oversized suitcase through a railway station and she shrank away. My friend said the woman had probably suspected him of trying to steal the luggage or demand payment for his help.

An antipathy that many people feel toward strangers, as described in Chapter 43, explains why some plead for help that they don't need. By contrast, those injured in Sichuan in the 2008 quake were regarded around China and much further afield as unwitting victims and truly desperate for help.

Generosity absolutely thrives in China when donors identify a bona fide need. Gift giving is already an enduring and complex part of Chinese culture. Gifts are exchanged at commonplace events, such as dinners, where people from Western countries such as mine would not think to make any such offerings. Presents in China should be physically large and sparkly—a sign that the giver cares about a receiver—while receivers are supposed to pretend it's nothing and open any wrapped boxes only later. I found all this out by giving small but, I imagined, useful gifts and asking recipients to open them on the spot. Some objects, such as clocks, make poor gifts because the Chinese word for a clock rhymes with "the end". But these exchanges apply mostly to people who know each other: family, friends and colleagues. Then there was the student who gave me, her university teacher, a new suede wallet before final exams. These acts normally answer calls to help family and other personal networks, a priority in China as outlined in Chapter 13. In the case of a student gifting a wallet, the act is a mild bribe. I took the wallet to be polite but have never used it.

Charity outside the personal network naturally extends the psychology of gifting. When exploring the literature on this topic, I found an Indiana University study saying donations reached 50.9 billion yuan in Mainland China in 2019, five times the 2007 total. The *Stanford Social Innovation Review* is more generous. It says charitable donations totaled 156 billion yuan in 2017, following compound annual growth of eleven percent from 2011 to 2016. The *Review* said at the end of 2016, China had 91 million individual donors, the world's fourth largest count, though still just seven percent of the population.

A lot of this rising sum comes from people, and sometimes companies, giving to popular causes through trusted channels. The Red Cross handily collects money, to wit: after the 2008 quake, though it has been criticized for not getting the money to its final destinations. Local governments have their own sway in marshalling donations. Local officials and the Red Cross have name recognition and, overall, a reputation for doing as pledged. They have mechanisms to vet as well whether the end-users of charity are legitimate or scammers.

But common people have shown their charitable side over the past few years more than ever through the internet, which allows for easy and anonymous donations.

Drawing again on the trust principle, donors are likely to give money online when a major, reputable company is handling transactions. Chinese internet icon Tencent raised 830 million yuan at its '99 Charity Day' in 2017, much of it through its ever-popular WeChat messaging app, according to *The Economist* news website. Fellow internet giant Alibaba in 2019 held a week's worth of activities to smooth charitable giving among its members and prompted about 500 volunteer organizations in 130 cities to join. Tencent and Alibaba are not just household names, but intimate ones for anyone who spends time online. They deliver what they promise when processing orders and payments. Neither one panhandles in Beijing.

A Law in Heaven and a Method on Earth

A sign outside the post office serving Beijing's chief diplomatic compound once read "no parking in this space." Cars parked there anyway. Customers and postal employees came and went without a glance. There are academics who filch passages from one another's papers and call the words their own, despite university policies that say don't. Cargo trucks aren't supposed to overload before taking a dangerous mountain highway from Inner Mongolia to Beijing, the law says. The trucks cram themselves with extra coal, accident risk aside, so they can rush it to energy-starved factories. These practices and a lot more like them all prove the Chinese idiom, 'a mandate in heaven and a method on earth'.

The axiom is required learning for survival in China. Otherwise, you will end up like me in my initial years in China — calling out breaches of posted rules and wondering why police and building security guards refuse to take action. Mandate-method gaps occur in much of the world. American highway drivers routinely cruise ten to twenty percent of the posted speed limits, for example. But the gap in China has expanded into a gaping chasm because leaders tend to find little advantage in enforcing sundry rules, while common people usually see more short-term good in flouting, rather than obeying them. Violators get away with most of their acts unless an authority wants to appear tough for a one-off reason, like looking concerned after the deadly spill of an overloaded truck.

Chinese vendors, therefore, are allowed to block many a narrow road despite fire hazard regulations. Plenty of those vendors have no sales permits. Gambling, technically illegal throughout China, thrives online. Employees are famous for reimbursing themselves from company kitties for private expenses. It's probably okay to park at will in front of the post office, regardless of posted signs.

The split between what's on paper and what's in practice frustrates quite a few expatriates who work with majority Chinese offices and Chinese business partners. The aggravation surges if they lead the Chinese staff of a company that's headquartered in a country with a smaller method-mandate gap. Office workers in China too often subvert in-house company SOPs to cut their hours or misspend their travel budgets. Chinese employees who outnumber foreign ones might operate on an unwritten, even unspoken code that specifies who does how much work and who gets what share of any company revenues that the boss doesn't know about.

I got an inkling of these workplace subtleties while working at China Daily. I would tell reporters periodically to add information or double-check sources. Sometimes they said in response that no more work could be done. Technically, they could have looked into my queries but knew they could opt out because someone else in the office had tacitly said it was okay to ignore the foreign editors.

Chinese philosophers going back several centuries BC

extoll the importance of following the mandate of 'heaven' — a religiously agnostic term referring to higher powers. The mandate is an ideal, a set of principles handed down to humans. Earthly rulers are supposed to enforce the mandate or face punishment. But heaven just issues broad suggestions, not strict lists of rules. People on earth are supposed to make the rules. As I read in a legal analysis by the Jones Day law firm, Chinese laws 'suffer from an overwhelming lack of clarity' and 'inevitably leave open large areas of ambiguity and uncertainty'.

Earthly rulers wherever they may be concern themselves mainly with taking, keeping and expanding power. In authoritarian countries such as China, leaders sometimes secure power by ignoring mandates except for the ones that ensure they stay in office. To enforce others would take time away from expanding their power and even cramp power by confining leadership activities to set rules rather than loftier objectives. Their subjects have been expected to form de facto self-policing networks, a facet of Chinese dynastic history.

Strict rules would help the lower ranks at least to stay free from any prosecution. These subjects could point to set rules and say I followed this, that and the other one. Leaders of the type outlined above prefer to keep channels open to prosecute quickly and freely, law-abiding people who just happen to be political opponents. For the leaders, rules would just get in the way.

Law-abiding subjects generally get used to the mandate-method duality if they grow up with it and learn handily to accommodate both heaven and earth. At the university where I taught in Beijing circa 2003, this one particularly English communications major was famous for passing all classes despite zero study and low assignment scores. Teachers were told to pass him because his mother worked for the university. I learned from letters to my Beijing newspaper Q&A column that other students win scholarships because of their personal connections with the veteran teachers. That was the method. The mandates, of course, say relentless study should generate high grades and confer scholarships.

Posted library rules on campus often forbid leaving unattended books and backpacks in study cubicles, but students do it anyway to tell classmates, "Stay away because this space is occupied." Passers-by in need of study spaces comply with the unwritten method, not the rules, and look for other seats if there are any. The students who have left their stuff behind are off eating lunch or attending class.

A lot of university students, coming off the life-should-be-fair ideals of adolescence, at first feel outraged by these violations. But the outrage usually fades once they too start leveraging connections for scholarships and realizing how convenient it is to leave their own books behind in the library. Later on, they'll understand that violations of mandates are about the only choice. Drivers who follow all posted rules in congested rush hours would add so much time to their trips it could truly be quicker to leave their workbenches at 9:00 p.m., three hours after normal quitting time, to wait for lighter traffic. If a worker submits only accurate expenses to a boss, while colleagues are inflating theirs with bogus receipts, the colleagues could worry that the honest one might snitch.

Who doesn't need a bit of this 'grey income'? Despite strong headline GDP figures and a fast-emerging middle class, salaries remain modest compared to mortgages, medical bills and adult children's tuition. These expenses lure workers into not-so-heavenly schemes, such as the padding reimbursement claims, to make extra money.

Many Chinese still quietly respect the mandate of heaven

even while snubbing it day to day. I've been surprised by looks of awe or snippets of praise for common displays of civility such as holding a door for strangers. University teachers who avoid favoring particular students in a class gain genuine respect because students value fairness in a leader. An employee who shuns the office receipt scam gets quiet admiration among colleagues, as long as she proves not to be a snitch. People regard morality as a foundation for the harmonious society that has eluded China for centuries but it is still held up as a policy goal. They follow the cruder earthly methods mainly to get ahead in a climate of chronic uncertainty.

New or Old? One Right Answer

Exit the old, enter the new. Nearly every new homeowner spends a stack of yuan on remodeling. Most shopkeepers renovate their stores before the grand opening. Even the emperor's Forbidden City compound in Beijing has been rebuilt several times—not quite the unshakable landmark that tourists take it to be. The latest idea to rebuild the Forbidden City came up in the 1960s, but the compound of imperial architecture was later declared a UNESCO World Heritage site and planners were barred from making big structural changes. Throughout the country, bikes are eagerly cast aside for cars, smartphones with technical problems get replaced with the latest model rather than fixed and even e-mail addresses are changed purely for the head rush of having something brand new.

New crushes old because new offers bodily comforts and a rise in social status that's pegged to money. Those advantages matter now after decades of socio-economic hard times.

On the pursuit of basic comforts: older Chinese flats have barren cement floors, crumbling brick walls and leaks that let in freezing, dusty air. Single-family 'ping fang' houses in the countryside tend to sprout the same problems. Commuting by bike, once the norm in flat cities such as Beijing, gets tiring especially in smog and vicious traffic. An engine, an upholstered seat and a shell of metal have obvious appeal to the haggard pedal turner. As a one-time Beijing bike rider, I recall the mouthfuls of bus exhaust and the motorists making sudden, illegal right turns through the city-designated cycling lanes.

Social status, another perk of sporting new stuff, normally derives from money. Those who can get something new must be able to afford it, earning the aspirational respect of poorer people who want the same thing — especially if it brings physical comforts. Chinese are fond of ascribing status to one another. That way they feel that an otherwise murky world around them follows a certain social order. The search for order descends from Confucianism, as noted in Chapter 34, and other Asian societies value wealth as a status sign largely for this same reason.

When the family upstairs starts a home remodelling project, the people below may quickly grow envious and hope they too will someday have enough money to afford wooden floors and modern kitchen equipment. To upgrade one's home is a rite of passage in modern China, and developers sell flats as empty boxes knowing just about every buyer will want to customize the whole thing from floor to ceiling. This surge in social status gives home remodelers license to blast, drill and hammer 24-7 — with few if any noise complaints — in the name of replacing old with new. By the same logic, the purchase of a new BMW earns status among onlookers who are tiring of their VW Jetta's (or bicycles).

Housing developers do much of their marketing based on people's thirst for comfort and status. They welcome prospective buyers with flashy facades, gaudy grand piano-furnished lobbies and freshly painted apartment interiors to create an aura of super-rich living. Like so many before me, I've walked into these lobbies and assumed that the units for sale are built to the same exquisite detail. Excited shoppers are supposed to feel so swept away they don't inquire about plumbing and the electrical wiring because no one can see those gritty innards — which don't boost a homeowner's status. Developers often use cheap yet flashy materials to save money and take building-code shortcuts to save time. Homes of this poor quality naturally breed structural issues within a few years, for example, the odour of other people's toilets transmitted through shared pipes.

My assumptions about a building's end-to-end quality based on room décor ended the day when I covered the news about a lawsuit filed by a group of Beijing homeowners. At a time when such civil cases were rare, they were suing their developer to seek payment for structural problems in their sparkling new apartment tower.

In one of the biggest out-with-the-old campaigns in modern history, Beijing's pre-Olympic Games demolition craze wiped out millions of square meters and displaced at least 1.5 million people. So profound was the change that today's inhabitants describe the capital in two phases — 'before the Games' and 'after the Games'.

Before the 2001 Olympics bid, single-story stone courtyard houses lined narrow lanes at the Beijing city centre. Low-rise brick apartment complexes inspired by Soviet architecture formed a ring around them. A bit of that Beijing gave way to sports venues and athletes' housing. But most tracts demolished before 2008 were turned into high-rise housing, shopping malls, wider roads and glassy offices for a population that would top 21 million. The Games provided a catalyst to tear down more than needed, satiating a fondness for the new and a thirst to improve appearances. The trend eventually spread all over urban China, spawning protests among displaced homeowners. I wrote stories about this urban metamorphosis in Beijing and

Shanghai. Although I met protesters who wanted to preserve older buildings as a living memory of the past, I found many more who just wanted a higher sum from redevelopers who were taking over their land through eminent domain. The average urbanite saw the replacement of buildings as a sign that China was moving toward a wealthier future—a mass sense of ridding the tired and the old for comfort, wealth and status.

Western interlopers are quick to question the demolition, the abandonment of bikes and the slow suburban creep afforded by mass automobile use. Older tracts of Beijing symbolized its careful masonry, wood working and courtyard design, these foreigners have argued. Cycling is healthy and cuts pollution. Traditional Chinese people normally reply that anything new functions better and should be more comfortable than anything old. I used to be one of those sceptical foreigners. I had my exchanges with local people and dug down to the coldly logical truth: they don't want to preserve reminders of China's long past of living in physical discomfort and wonder whether Western preservationists want Chinese to keep living as poor now as they did in the past. To retrofit older buildings with modern comforts would require ongoing maintenance costs as well as initial capital. This retrofit process in the end would not deliver the sense of leapfrog improvement conferred by a whole new structure.

The owners of Victorian houses in San Francisco offer a big contrast. They spend money as needed to keep their circa-1850 houses solid and comfortable because San Franciscans regard them as historic treasures. Unlike much of China, San Francisco is packed with money, both old and new. Homeowners can afford retrofits, maintenance and a lot more. More significantly, they are not refugees from decades-plus of cheap, uncomfortable housing. Instead they believe an old home comes with the same comfort and status as a new one.

Chinese people do, on the whole, value historic architecture as relics of their old and enduring culture. This sentiment is in fact growing. Developers have accordingly built detailed replicas of the destroyed architecture in cities such as Beijing. These faux-old structures now form districts with so much structural uniformity that some feel more like theme parks than neighborhoods. An example is the Qianmen district near Tiananmen Square in Beijing. Qianmen re-emerged from full-blown redevelopment in 2011 as a tourist zone with a dedicated streetcar. It's got comfy toilets and air conditioning that were harder to come by before. It advances Beijing's collective status as a modern city.

Medication: Anything Will Do if You Believe in It

Virtually all medical treatments are welcome in China if they have worked, might work or are said to work. Anxious people can be seen lining up at pharmacies for creams to ease mosquito bites. Among the patients who pack hospital waiting rooms, some will be formally diagnosed with only the common cold a given a small shopping bag's worth of prescription medications. I heard of one case in which a surgeon offered to remove a patient's uterus to resolve a bacterial infection. The doctor was surprised when his patient raised questions about the risk of failure and asked for meds instead. These vignettes point to deep trust in physicians and Western medicine, even as many Westerners increasingly opt for bed rest, fluids and just toughing it out. At the same time, I've found, China's 2,500-year-old traditional medicine enjoys healthy popularity. The Chinese formulas are usually taken to prevent disease while the foreign stuff is used to treat it. Ginger, herbs and roots are among the preventive formulas. They're sold in expensive parts of cities and get plenty of customers. Beyond that, many Chinese embrace medically unrecognized folk practices such as avoidance of ice and sponging sweat off their necks immediately after exercise—both done to prevent upper respiratory diseases.

Fear of sudden illness, lack of faith in public health systems and a pragmatic sense of trying anything that might work anchor this eager acceptance of multiple remedies. Low incomes raise the appeal of cheaper solutions and the quest to come home from doctor's visits with bags full of pills they might never use. Some groups outside China with the same fears, public health pitfalls and practical outlook feel the same way, though China stands out for its system of traditional medicine.

The specter of serious illness or injury is real. Centuries of grimy poverty pre-1980s, and tough blue-collar labor genuinely raised the risk of health problems in China. As shown by the 2003 severe acute respiratory syndrome (SARS) outbreak and possibly by the origin of Covid-19, sanitation, population density and climate peculiarities in China easily fan new viruses. Memories of close relatives getting sick and dying young still weigh on numerous modern Chinese people, who in turn may chronically worry about disease.

Chinese citizens typically fear that whatever health insurance they have won't cover major hospital care, because earlier in their lifetimes it probably didn't. Therefore, many prepare 'red envelope' cash for their doctors as security for prompt, effective treatment. Lower-income households probably can't afford those payments, so they veer toward cheap, accessible home remedies and getting all the medication possible from any out-of-pocket doctor's visits. A bag of pills from the pharmacy after a visit says too that a patient has done everything possible about a disease, regardless of how minor.

Doctors may privately know that a lot of their prescriptions are unnecessary. I panicked once when my elementary school-aged younger daughter had vomited for two days and started losing weight. We went to pediatrics at the closest hospital and sat in a waiting room with another 50 patients until the doctor called her number. He had been processing colds and upset stomachs all day, giving each kid about two minutes of his time to clear the queue. The doctor saw I was a foreigner and asked me whether in my country so many people would report to a hospital for such minor conditions. I asked him not to bother with meds — and my daughter started to feel better that day on her own.

At the public healthcare level, disease prevention improves but remains spotty. Mosquito abatement is still relatively rare, for example. Before the 2020 coronavirus outbreak, so was the routine sterilization of objects likely to be contaminated. Common people as well as local health departments could do more collectively to make their environs healthier, but generally no one steps up to the cause. For that reason, spaces such as schoolyards and railway stations trend dirty. As noted in previous chapters, Chinese may regard one another as rivals rather than cohorts in creating a better society. The same ethos explains the lack of upkeep of shared buildings and inattention to safety hazards.

On the pragmatic side, prescription medications from a famous pharmaceutical company get respect because they are stronger, better tested and more time-proven in multiple countries than other solutions. Traditional medicine for disease prevention is proven in China, sustaining its popularity. Tricks such as the avoidance of ice appeal to people with less education and without the money for formally recognized medications.

The least attention goes to bed rest, rehydration and a low-stress lifestyle. Those solutions don't feel emphatic enough when something else out there can attack a disease head on. Hardware such as pills happens to be more popular than software such as rest not only for healthcare. Traditional parents prefer private lessons (hard) over letting children learn through play (soft). New buildings get more public approval than urban green space because construction feels harder, more real and shows China is going places. Back to health, many prefer a face shield (hard) over social distancing (softer) as an anti-Covid measure.

The root of Chinese medicine comes down to vital energy flows in the human body or 'qi' (sometimes spelled 'chi'). This energy connects different bodily forces. It can be disrupted by muscle tension, poor diet or excessive negative thinking. Because of its all-embracing nature, qi has become something of a proxy for overall health. And being so broad, qi has undergone major word-of-mouth reinterpretation such as if someone drinks this or that, it will improve qi, even if it doesn't. These para-scientific or outright unscientific ideas get passed on without debate from one generation to the next, like any other enduring element of a culture. For that reason, many Chinese believe untested elixirs, foods and lifestyle habits have medical properties.

I gave myself a mini medical school course for this chapter by reading the relevant section of Charles Windridge's *Tong Sing: The Know Everything Book* on China. It lists twenty-five foods and spices said to have health benefits apart from ordinary nutrition. Garlic is a blood cleanser, for example. Coriander inhibits aging. Thyme 'eradicates wrinkles'. Windridge calls some of these claims "magical", with "efficacy that is often exaggerated".

The 2003 SARS outbreak in Beijing showed the power of word-of-mouth recommendations for cheap health boosters. A badminton rage captured the city that spring because so many people thought sports would strengthen immunity against the deadly lung disease. Most apartment complexes had yard space for badminton nets, making the sport accessible and cheap. Within weeks, families all over Beijing were stringing up nets.

The uncomfortable truth: athletes catch viruses just about like everyone else.

The government keeps improving sanitation and disease prevention work but unless faced with a massive threat such as famine, SARS or the coronavirus outbreak, Chinese leaders still tend to treat the health of individual people as a tertiary matter beyond the state's purview. But citizens seldom fault government, because they never expected official support. They've got their own medical war chests ready, and anything could be inside.

What Chinese Think of Foreigners and How Foreigners Can Adapt

The non-Asian tourist arriving at a Chinese provincial railway station turns every head in the arrival hall. But hardly anyone will talk to a foreigner when an Asian friend, spouse or colleague is traveling alongside. Non-Asians stand out like pumpkins in schooners of white rice. They are presumed as well to be ignorant of the Chinese language due to race, while their Asian counterparts are credited as totally fluent even if they're Japanese. Many in China resent foreigners whose governments create rows with their own. Yet Chinese have a reputation among expatriates for chasing foreigners to sell things, practice English, do business and even get married. I've experienced all of the above as a white guy.

Each transaction points to a different angle from which Chinese commonly see foreign visitors and expatriates. The recurring themes: curiosity, usefulness, distrust and national pride.

First, a definition of 'foreigner'. The common thinking in China divides people not born in China into three broad categories. One comprises white people, people of African ancestry, Latin

Americans and Middle Easterners. Chinese may refer to them plaintively (yet inoffensively) as 'wai guo ren' or 'lao wai', where 'wai' means outside, 'guo' country, 'ren' people and 'lao wai' means old outsider'. To them, these people are truly different from the Chinese because they look different and come from far-off lands. A second category is other East Asians, who are not seen as true foreigners, but as ethnic extensions of the Chinese who speak other languages because they live outside China. Wealthier Asians, such as Japanese and South Koreans are given a wary, competitive eye, plus admiration for cultural products such as Korean television drams. The third type is ethnic Chinese born or naturalised somewhere outside China, from Singapore to San Francisco. Inhabitants of China like to see them as wholly Chinese in terms of language, culture and identity.

This chapter covers mainly foreigners in the far-off land category. Because they look, talk and act differently than locals, these newcomers get stared at (more on staring in Chapter 43). Foreigners get the most stares in parts of China where locals aren't used to seeing them, for example, in working-class inland cities such as Datong and Nanchang. Staring seldom has ill intent, incidentally. Once a foreigner smiles at the googly-eyed other party, a smile usually comes back. That said, it gets to be too much. After walking around central Nanchang for a couple of hours one morning and getting pierced by about every third pair of eyeballs, I went back to my hotel and stayed there until my bus to the airport left the next day.

Lack of understanding is the catalyst for curiosity as well as some of the snubbing that foreigners experience in daily encounters. People with no East Asian ancestry who sit down with a Chinese-slash-other Asian friend at a restaurant and order in Chinese are likely to be ignored. Most wait staffers reply only to the friend because he must know Chinese as an Asian, whereas the speaker as a non-Asian can't know. Ditto for foreigners, accompanied by Chinese-looking friends, who ask directions and meet socially with local people. Foreigners trying to interact on their own, with no friend, are usually taken more seriously. But they fetch some leave-me-alone smiles and dismissive waves of the hand for fear they can't communicate—due to race. A lot of people believe Chinese is too tough for outsiders to master. A few even say openly that "you're simple and we're complex." They might point to an estimated 4,000 to 5,000 years of Chinese civilization. Many switch to English, even if the foreigner is fluent in Chinese and the other person can say just a few dozen English words. I've tested my case here by wearing a black cap outside to hide my non-Asian hair color and making phone calls to avoid being seen at all. Chinese people I encounter in these setups will assume from my accent that I'm from a distant province, but still from China. They take me seriously and respond without looking for an Asian friend or switching languages.

Asians from other countries look Chinese, so they're expected to speak with full fluency. Ethnic Chinese from the West, if they can't speak Chinese, may be taken as disdainful of China and excessively proud of their home countries instead.

Chinese often assume too that white people live better than the majority in China because of average per capita income comparisons. For that reason, these visitors are potentially useful. Vendors are known for hounding foreigners to buy overpriced artwork in touristy parts of Beijing. Foreigners are approached on university campuses for informal exchanges of Chinese and English lessons. Some don't bother with the exchange—just go straight into the English. I recall one chat in the lobby of a Peking University library. Two students introduced themselves in shaky, grade-C English at a time when I was already tired of being used for my native language. I replied in Chinese, which was no better than their English. We conversed that way for a long time, with neither of us conceding a single sentence in our own native language. Particularly ambitious English speakers occasionally target foreigners for support in applying for visas, imagining that average citizens can walk into their embassies and sort out documentation on behalf of someone else. A few Chinese women and some Chinese men approach foreigners for marriage so they can go through him to get a visa.

Distrust of foreigners shows when China's government gets into a row with another country, especially a big one. Targeted countries usually include Australia, Japan, the United States and the larger Western European nations. Most Chinese throw aside any inter-city and inter-provincial rivalries to band together in the face of perceived external threats. The government has nurtured people through formal schooling and mass media to believe its interests are uniform with the people's. Common Chinese usually assume foreigners have the same relationship with their own leaders through the media in their homelands. Foreigners would all but uniformly back their governments, the assumption continues.

When US missiles hit the Chinese embassy in Belgrade in May 1999 during NATO's war against the former Yugoslavia, China disputed the US claim of an accident. China's outrage resonated deeply with the population. I was told by expatriates who reached Beijing before I did, which was late 1999, that taxi drivers upset about the bombing would ignore white passengers who tried to flag them down. An American friend who had accepted a job with the English-language *China Daily* newspaper that year told me he asked the newspaper's personnel office before arriving in Beijing whether he would be safe in public. He said the office sent back only an e-mail saying it supported the Chinese government's view that the embassy bombing was intentional. In 2001, a US spy plane flew near China's south coast, a Chinese pilot died trying to chase it and the US crew was interrogated after making an emergency landing in China. I met an American IT worker who apologized to his Chinese colleagues who were giving him heat. His statement closed the case because he was taken as a proxy for the White House.

Foreigners from relatively poor countries get stared at. But locals seldom chase, grill or surveil them as those foreigners look neither like sources of economic opportunity nor threats to China.

Still, thanks to long-standing restrictions on foreign travel and constant chatter about other countries that are covered lavishly (though not always accurately) in the media, Chinese often feel deeply curious about what foreigners are up to. For this reason, Sino-foreign friendships are easy to cement. Some of the people who approach foreigners for personal gain can be channelled into ordinary friends even if the initial encounter is a bumpy one. The one-time outsider might eventually meet the friend's friends too on the way to building a network of normal, not-too-aggressive, not-so-nationalistic, Chinese-speaking Chinese people. They'll still want advice on learning English and brood when other governments spar with China's. Most of the time, however, they're just common friends. For me, they've become the earth, fire and water of my years in China.

Shoving, Spitting, Staring and Driving

Spitting in public after a noisy, throaty windup. Yelling in pure excitement. Mobbing ticket counters and crowding train platforms so thick that arriving passengers can't get off. Then there's the chewing with mouths open, the smoking next to strangers and the staring at people who don't look Asian. So common are these habits in China that Chinese travel agencies have implored their citizens to change their behavior to make better impressions while touring overseas.

Most Chinese people don't have these habits. They're observant, sanitary and respectful of how their actions affect people around them. My friends in Beijing all belong to this growing majority of the Chinese population. But enough people still spit, shout and stare that one need not venture outside for long to see them.

Coarse public behavior persists largely because China is still building a civil society (Chapter 20 explains where civil society stands). Parents aplenty implore their children to respect bosses, teachers and influential friends because those non-family outsiders provide material opportunities. Strangers could seize those opportunities, so many people distrust or disrespect others outside their families, a carryover from historic competition for scarce resources that continues now due to China's population size and people's modern ambitions. This contemptuous lack of concern for society would leave little incentive to mind manners. (The kind of organized religion that might prescribe cleaner behavior has sat out much of Chinese history.) Tense classrooms and workplaces in China compound some people's urge to Let. It. Rip. after hours, say, by shouting and staring when out with friends in a restaurant.

Citizens who consider underlying reasons for public behavior often point to China's ongoing economic development, assuming that social graces naturally come with more money. They correctly argue that if everyone's sure about having money, fewer people should panic about getting things to the point of offending strangers. I once had this debate with a Beijing-born co-worker and asked her about Southeast Asia, where resources are scarcer than China's but where most local people shun crude acts in public. Filipinos seldom stare; Laotians aren't known for spitting all over their sidewalks. She acknowledged something unique to China but didn't know quite what.

Chinese friends of mine have, however, pointed out a connection between crude public behavior and society's intense competition for resources, whether that's time or train tickets. This link could explain why many in China still act on fear that if they don't push through a crowd or jump a queue, they won't be able to get whatever scarce item is for sale, because multiple strangers are gunning for the same thing at whatever expense needed. I once saw a tangle of about fifty people all but crushing one another at the Taiyuan railway station to reach a ticket counter and get seats on a train to Beijing. The train was leaving soon and tickets might sell out. I've seen plenty of pedestrians push past one another on sidewalks rather than doing the "you go first" dance that's common in other countries. What's the hurry? The pusher arrives at work on time; the pushed is late and looks bad among peers.

Traffic opportunism ranks among the more obvious coarse behaviors, in my observations as a bus passenger, taxi customer, cyclist and pedestrian: cars stop in crosswalks and drive on sidewalks. Buses might slalom in front of smaller vehicles to cut them off for a right turn. Cars park in bus stops if other curbside spaces are full. Passengers at the stop sometimes can't see past the bulkier parked cars to tell whether their bus is coming. Pedestrians and people on two-wheeled transport normally just yield.

The cars, buses and pedestrians described here are unwittingly taking stock of their relative speeds and sizes to decide their moves. According to this hierarchy, pedestrians as the smallest and slowest, should stop for cars in mid-crosswalk, even when the walk signal is on. They hardly ever complain because they're all following an unwritten yet rigid and time-tested social order that humans without civil society observe when under pressure: size matters and get out of the way if you're small. Competition again fuels this pattern. Other people on the road can grab your space and time if you don't outmaneuver them. This social order works because traffic rule enforcement is weak in much of China.

Then there's a bit of rage, on road and off. A week of work or study can be especially intense in China. Teachers might scold students who speak in error as classmates snicker, so the average face-conscious student keeps as quiet as possible. In offices, trusted co-workers message one another to avoid being overheard by supervisors and less trusted peers, breeding a tensely quiet workspace. Whether in class or at work, the risk of embarrassment from saying a thing or two keeps a lot of ideas pent up in the brain cells. I've asked my own students in

China why they won't speak out in class when they know their material. It's fear of someone else's reaction, they tell me. For these reasons, when people go out for fun, an obvious number of them thrive on commotion. Quite a few groups of office employees scream and clap their hands at jokes when they go out after work on Fridays. Children may be allowed to get up from restaurant tables to run around, even at the risk of barging into other customers and waiters carrying hot soup tureens.

Government agencies do post signs urging citizens to be kinder and sometimes threaten to fine violators. Yet fines are rare. Spitting, shoving and aggressive driving do not soil the state's ability to govern. Public security offices still shutter social media forums that could unite groups of strangers behind a cause. The lack of forums leaves people disconnected save for family and friends, prolonging distrust of the outer world.

But society is strengthening on its own. As I read in scholar Shi Yin-hong's study, 'The Issue of Civil Society in China and its Complexity', an 'embryonic' civil society is taking shape as Chinese people earn money without help from the state and learn from business partners overseas how other societies work (through a trade association, for example). In the biggest cities, particularly around universities and office districts dominated by people under 40, coarse behaviour is already rare. Trust among strangers emerges fast in these enclaves due to everyone's shared experience — countering competition — and the lack of scarce basic resources in their adult lifetimes. A student probably wouldn't cut in line right in front of a fellow student. But their elders had to fight for food just 60 years ago and some still wonder whether their share of the goods might get taken if they don't scramble to the front of the line first.

Non-Violence as a Strict Code for Handling Disputes

The Chinese government, its mass media and a lot of common people have no shortage of comments about how China lacks the gun violence of the United States. The relative lack of random violence lifts as well the spirits of China-based foreigners who had avoided going out at night in their homelands. Late-night bar districts flourish in multiple parts of Beijing and Shanghai and it's okay to pass out drunk in the street until dawn with little risk other than an errant pickpocket and an angry police officer who will spirit the sot indoors. I freely biked all over Beijing once I realized there was no such thing as a violent ghetto, quite a shock after living in large US cities. Chinese seldom assault strangers out of anger or for personal gain.

Violence is widely seen as a last resort to solving a problem. Violence reflects a person's lack of self-control, which is a prized virtue. Some people know too they can assuage anger and even get revenge more effectively than through physical force.

Reasons for equals keeping their hands off one another date back to when the influential scholar Confucius said violence should be reserved for soldiers with years of experience plus the right to carry arms. If someone starts a fight, after all, the same someone had best be strong enough to finish it without the risk of reprisal. The scholar saw violence as a solution, usually for the military, only when no other means could solve a dire dispute.

That was 2,500 years ago. More enduring reasons for China's pervasive non-violence reflect fears of a long-term loss of face that could jeopardize chances to marry well and hold China's best jobs. To lash out physically places one at the bottom of China's list of maladaptive qualities. Violence implies rash, sloppy thinking that culminates in an obviously risky move. I've noticed that when a child throws a tantrum, parents are quicker to scold him into shutting up than to figure out what's wrong. They're giving the kid a life lesson: don't come off as wild and crazy. To save face further, Chinese seldom cry in public, even with family. Instead, they grin when angry to say, "The horrid situation I'm facing doesn't get me down." Chapter 36 has more on this point.

Single people, along with their parents, want mates who can shoulder setbacks such as job losses and family financial strain with resilience and a can-do attitude. At work, connections often matter more than excelling at a skillset. Employers may lack transparent rules about pay, time off and promotions. So, it makes more sense to shower a boss with kindness rather than tip over a bookshelf and throw a laptop in response to a demotion. That kind of magnanimity leads to a future promotion. It's no wonder that fathers in China don't teach their children to fight in school. That training is a facet of many Western families.

In the book research phase of this chapter, I found a 2017 study published in a US National Library of Medicine journal. It says Chinese men are less likely than British men to be violent toward members the general population. It found, however, that a higher percentage of Chinese men acted violently toward their intimate partners. While no one encourages domestic violence, it's the non-domestic kind that would make strangers feel unsafe and travel guidebooks write down a city as dangerous. The study found too that British men learned violence in childhood and felt confident in their ability to fight. For them, it said, violence is 'acceptable behaviour'.

One day at an upscale Beijing restaurant, a drunken man lobbed an empty liquor bottle at me after making a few loud, uncouth comments about foreigners. I was two tables way and the bottle missed, but his throw shook the other restaurant guests and waitresses into silence. No one, however, tried to stop him from throwing more bottles because they didn't need to. As drunk as he was, the man knew after just one outburst that everyone else in the restaurant saw him as a violator of China's non-violence code.

But Chinese do widely respect aggressors who exact revenge for their anger in clever, nonviolent ways. Someone who is mad enough to break out a knife (Chinese seldom carry guns) can probably come up with an even scarier way to get even after suppressing rage long enough to plot a scheme.

One common solution: forming a posse of friends, even a hired gangster, to track down the offender and make a threat strong enough that the other party backs down. When four or five guys suddenly surround an offender, the offender usually caves without a fight. This conflict resolution method contributed to the rise of triads in Hong Kong and Taiwan. Gangs flourish in Mainland China, too, but lack the cinematic fame their Hong Kong counterparts enjoy. People with enough money might ask the gang to protect them as well against any counter-reprisals from the other party.

Longer-term revenge plots may grow so effective that an offender doesn't know what happened until revenge is complete. Someone angered to the point of blind rage by a co-worker, for example, will spread rumors behind the offender's back over several months and urge co-workers do to the same. The same coterie of co-workers would follow up by withholding information, such as news about an unposted but important staff meeting. The undesirable becomes isolated, suspicious and unable to do much work.

Some dwellers among the eight-digit populations of Beijing and Shanghai live in districts of tattered one-room brick houses near the railway tracks. They might work in menial jobs or be out hunting for those jobs. Perhaps they drink and get mad at life. Some turn to pickpocketing and petty theft. And violent crimes do occur. In 2018, a jeep packed with explosives drove into a crowd on the Beijing tourist landmark Tiananmen Square. Two civilians were killed along with the driver and two passengers. That same year, China had logged an eight-year-long string of mass stabbings and cleaver attacks in public places. They had killed a combined total of twenty-five people. But for the most part, day by average day, China has the right to gloat about the lack of violence.

Policing Where Law Is Third Priority

Rampant, routine violations of the most ordinary rules defy China's international stereotype as a place rife with crackdowns. Cars drive on sidewalks, despite codes that say don't. Unlicensed vendors form ad hoc malls on curbs, though the spaces are not approved for guerrilla sales. Police officers watch a lot of these violations unfold in front of them without making a move. I've seen a few vendor busts. When I've been able to watch one until the end, I've noticed that vendors start returning after the officers leave the bust site.

Reasons for this apparently lax policing are best summed up by the common three-word phrase for relations between violators and enforcers: 'qing li fa'. It means 'feeling, principle, law', with some variation depending on who you ask'". Law enforcers in China, from police to building managers and environmental protection authorities, usually handle transgressions in that order.

'Qing li fa' came about because over the centuries Chinese lacked a strict, elaborate code of laws enshrined on paper, I've come to understand through book research. Instead, they had situations to be sorted out by clan elders, who acted largely on principle and gut feeling. A series of dynasties encouraged a 'bao jia' law enforcement system whereby groups of families shared responsibility for crimes committed by any of their members. I noticed from a passage in Arthur Smith's book *Chinese Characteristics* that says neighbors too would take responsibility as well for someone's wrong, on the assumption they should know one another's behavior intimately due to living nearby. The informal system worked especially well because people aligned more back then with clans and villages than with a broader force that might impose rules. Informal self-policing remains common in a lot of agrarian or village-based societies in the world. In China, the scheme has freed formal law enforcement agents over the centuries to pursue top-drawer violent crimes and acts that threaten the power of rulers.

Law coming in third place today hardly means that the books allow anyone to do anything. China has a library's worth of codes with an elaborate taxonomy of 'laws', 'regulations', legal 'clauses' and other do-and-don't descriptors that the English language struggles to capture. Police officers under China's Ministry of Public Security have full authority to enforce this matrix of rules.

Situations, another plausible translation for the first word in 'qing li fa', normally start with a complaint. Because police officers tend to wait for complaints before opening a case, they seldom stop petty violations that they just happen to see on patrol. Without a complaint, there's no situation. Seasoned officers know crimes hurt people whom they can't see or who withhold complaints for fear of getting dragged into a messy case. But the superiors of those officers seldom require enforcement of misdemeanor-level laws without complaints.

Once a victim complains, most officers listen attentively, ask ample questions and take pages of notes. I filed a noise complaint against a Beijing neighbor who hammered and drilled week after week outside the building management's posted hours for remodeling. Two officers came to my building, heard me out and spoke to the building manager. Site managers represent another type of rule-enforcer in China. In my case, the building manager agreed to pursue the violator but ultimately said the guy wouldn't change his remodeling crew's work hours. Police officers who believe a situation to be relatively serious, perhaps threatening a wider group of citizens, would normally proceed from the report to contacting suspects who they can easily reach and may pressure them to make confessions. My case didn't make it and the two officers never followed up, to my knowledge. The remodeling went on and on. A police chief is unlikely to require an investigation into a small, one-off case such as mine at the expense of solving higher-profile crimes.

Chinese citizens alleging illegal seizure of their property by government-backed developers, a hallmark of the large-scale demolition outlined in Chapter 40, have told me in news interviews police won't even take their cases. The government would oppose any action against its developers and that's final. There's no situation.

Principle, sometimes translated instead as 'logic', is second in the 'qing li fa' series. When enforcers take cases to this level, they step in more as arbitrators of fairness and reasonableness than as arbiters of whether someone broke a law. Let's say lots of people complain a remodeling project is exceeding hours set by the city government—so many people that local media are starting to check it out (even if they're not allowed to report). A situation has taken shape. The officer, invoking principle, could decide here, after hearing out both sides, what the remodeler and angry neighbors should do, based on what each side says. Even if the law says stop at 10:00 p.m., an officer might suggest that the remodelers finish that single day's work at 11:00 p.m. because they're almost done with a phase of a project that would be costly to set up again the next day. No one gets penalized. When public security bureaus recover stolen property, they often don't chase the thieves, just hand belongings back to the owners. All belongings have ended up in the right hands, satisfying another principle: fairness.

Principle leans toward haves over have-nots, a simple way of ordering society by status as described in previous chapters. More assets mean more respect and higher odds of a favorable decision by rule enforcers. According to this tenet, shopkeepers come out ahead of angry customers. Developers prevail over owners of individual flats in their buildings. It's less important who flouted the rules. Foreigners are taken extra seriously as victims in China's few violent crime cases because of their potential weight in foreign relations. They could create diplomatic problems for China if their cases are unsolved.

Taking principle (and haves versus have-nots) to a higher level, political scholars have argued police work today primarily to protect the state, its interests and its image. Officers of the law, they believe, wait for directives from up the ranks somewhere, such as, "We have a delegation from the United States today, so get rid of all the roadside peddlers of illegally copied software this week." I heard this line from political science experts whom I interviewed for news stories when crackdowns on copyright piracy were a big thing in China around 2000. China would have looked bad when the copyright-conscious Americans showed up and saw the peddlers, I was told. A senior Chinese leader might also order police to stop any photographers from approaching the scene of a recent riot and monitor movements of the former rioters. The government risks wider social unrest if rioting resumes. Rule enforcers use law, the third word in the 'qing li fa' series, last when gut sense and principle can't clear up a matter. Western people may expect officers to use the law first, regardless of who's who and the stories they tell. I fell into this trap as a newbie in China and wondered why police or at least building managers wouldn't halt noise violations spelled out under their own codes. A Chinese officer normally invokes the law when two parties of similar rank disagree on how to resolve, say, a car crash or a right-of-way dispute and disagree with the officer's principle-based suggestions.

Graft covers the whole 'qing li fa' trio. Acts such as using government money for private dinners and personal shopping trips have no obvious victim, so they pass the situation test. And is it really wrong in principle to hold banquets and buy name-brand European handbags with public funds? Many traditional Chinese, like peers in much of the world, believe high positions imply the right to take a bit more than an ordinary salary. But corruption was growing costly, so in 2013 the government used the law to order a wide-reaching crackdown that remains largely in effect today.

Why a Chinese Person Makes the Perfect Dinner Date

Dinner dates in China are serious events. People seldom flake out, turn up but say nothing or bring other people unannounced. If someone is running even ten minutes late, the other party gets a so-sorry text message and a burst of further apologies when that someone finally comes running into the restaurant lobby. Cancellations are rare except for genuine work and family emergencies. Even the stickiest wallflowers do their best to talk when seeing friends one on one. Hardly anyone monopolizes mealtime conversation. When it's time to pay, sometimes all parties jump up to be the first. So intense was that competition that I would sometimes fake a trip to the toilet before the end of a meal to sneak off and pay before anyone else could consider it.

This degree of commitment, compared with the casual get-togethers common in the West, reflects a search and respect for social order among Chinese. When seeing friends, colleagues, classmates, teachers and new acquaintances one-on-one, Chinese follow a code of etiquette that's based on old, universally understood social norms. The codes extend from teachings of the Chinese philosopher Confucius. He advocated that people observe status rankings from within the smallest unit, the family, on upward. The ranks ensured that everyone had a clear identity and clear duties, an antidote to the social disharmony and warlike chaos that China had already endured.

Confucius put into memorable language what everyone already knew: people in power are supposed to get respect from those without it, elders know more than youth and those of high status (including older age) have a duty to help the lower status for the human race to thrive. Today these codes give the modern Chinese a sense of order that overrides any temptation to bring an unannounced guest to a dinner or hog the conversation. Those with higher status should feel an obligation at the dinner table toward those without status, so they pay the bill. Equals at the table seek harmony. The codes give everyone there a sense of safety and predictability that can be hard to find in an otherwise opaque, hyper-competitive modern China.

It's not to say that every date is perfect. Traffic in China's oppressively urban cities such as Beijing make even the best time managers late. The lure of smartphones drains time from face-to-face conversation. Men sometimes get pressured to drink to the point of vomiting and wetting their trousers as they stagger around looking for a toilet. I won't mention any men by name, but one wrote this book. And if some poor soul at the table can't sing at least one song from start to finish, good-natured ridicule will surely follow. I'm no singer. I would pay my dues in Beijing by croaking out *99 Bottles of Beer* until table mates ordered me to stop around 96. At least we would all be laughing, for the right reasons.

Here are the code highlights:

First, whoever suggests a meal plans to pay, particularly for on-on-one meetings. Chinese delight in mocking Westerners for splitting bills, especially as coins spill across a restaurant table and each person tries to produce an equal amount of cash. They find that practice to be cold, hardly confirming of friendship.

Over time, bills tend to come out even anyway between two people of equal rank and age. Party A invites and pays today. Next time, party B suggests something and pays for it. The third time around, it's back to Party A. Groups of young university classmates and work colleagues make exceptions by splitting bills in recognition of their equal rank. It would be impractical to pass the cheque from person to person over multiple meals.

Second rule, people of higher social status should treat. That could mean a 65-year-old treats a 30-year-old, at least most of the time, even if they're just friends with no business relationship. Bosses, obviously higher status than their employees, usually pay for any food and entertainment enjoyed together, whether or not it's linked to work. Foreigners may find it hard to pay, as Chinese tend to see them as guests in the country deserving hospitality for newcomers, even if they have lived there for years. Groups — with higher status than a single person by virtue of number — usually treat individuals who are collectively invited. Upwards of twenty university students would periodically take me, their teacher, to dinner at the ends of semesters to show thanks, for example, or as a quiet plea for lenience in grading.

One university class in Beijing circa 2003 had treated me twice at mid-range Beijing restaurants. The bill was around 1,000 yuan each time for twenty people. The students divided it among themselves and the stuffed, drunk teacher paid nothing. As a higher-status person, the instructor had a right, even an obligation, to treat. But the students were stronger by volume. (I did eventually cover everyone in that particular class at a teahouse.)

Dinner rule No. 3, during conversation, start off with uncontroversial but meaty topics such as how work or school is going. One party's quick summary of her work, from pay grade to professional satisfaction, invites other parties to offer a supportive analysis. Then someone else talks about work. The speakers and listeners should be fishing for points of relationship-building harmony, for instance, that they want to change careers but hope to stay in Beijing. That moment of harmony, possibly consecrated with a toast, opens the gate to other matters.

Family updates is another safe topic: basic status checks on parents, spouses and children are shared, followed by encouraging tips and a search for common ground. Chinese who see someone as a friend generally don't hide harsh truths about work and family. They might tell a new acquaintance more than usual, in fact, because family members or closer friends would have strong biased views. Or they could spread gossip.

Later stages of a dinner discussion could veer into heady matters including politics. Most Chinese citizens have some kind of gripe against government, their own as well as others, and especially on domestic problems such as property market regulation and traffic jam relief. I found I need not worry as a foreigner about offending someone's patriotism by asking Chinese dinner guests about the severity of Beijing's air pollution or difficulty in getting railway tickets before a holiday. Often their complaints — on daily living upward to the affairs of state — would start without my even raising an issue at all.

Company milestones, especially recent staffing changes, keep the chatter going at typical office meals. In-house gossip is frequent. Hardly anyone talks too long — it's rude to deprive someone else of a chance to speak.

Fourth rule, expect fun. Longer, larger gatherings can quickly turn hyper-festive. Someone takes a good-natured jab at someone else, present or otherwise. Everyone else is supposed to laugh, the target if present jabs back and everyone laughs again. Larger group gatherings may centre around a group activity to show the host cares so much that he's added entertainment to the F&B. The most common activity: singing one by one karaoke-style and I don't mean 99 Bottles of Beer. Everyone normally takes a turn in the spirit of order and equal participation.

Why Superstition Has an Outsized Following

Superstition feels almost as rampant as rice in China. The Chinese concept of feng shui, an elaborate prescription for how to place objects in physical spaces such as the home, has generated enough intrigue to support how-to books written in English. The color red brings luck. Wedding reception guests should avoid giving clocks because the Chinese translation rhymes with 'end', as in the end of life. Use of fireworks at certain times and dates during the 14-day Lunar New Year period is supposed to protect the shooter from evil spirits and allow one's business to prosper over the coming twelve months. Material offerings to local gods or one's own ancestors loosely qualify as superstition, too.

People throughout the world have superstitions, to wit: Friday the thirteenth and black cats crossing one's path bringing bad luck. I personally distrust the whole month of March, because it historically brings an outsized barrage of bad news, perhaps for lack of major holidays that cheer up the world.

But in China the number of these beliefs and the fervor with which they're held stand out over many other countries. Superstition is a routine conversation topic in China and not a jocular one as it might be in a Western country. Even some people who profess no belief except the proven boundaries of science pray at temples and arrange their homes in honor of feng shui, which gives advice as granular as the placement of houseplants. They just feel safer that way, implying a level of trust in superstition.

Three reasons explain this devotion. First, China is demographically homogenous compared to a lot of other countries, creating extensive overlaps in people's life ambitions rather than a society with multiple, widespread definitions of success. Those who chase success a-la-majority may derive a burst in confidence, if not real help, by obeying a superstition their peers might have neglected. The second thing, a widespread belief in collective agency, rather than reliance on oneself only, extends to the supernatural. That means adherence to superstition would invite spirits to one's own camp, while neglecting them would upset the spirits. The third reason, superstitions promote at least the illusion that knotty problems can be fixed fast, offering an elusive sense of personal control in a fluctuating, opaque country.

Outliers abound in China as anywhere. But similar ambitions are more numerous. Most people would agree, for example, that making money is their top priority just out of college—compared say to a year in the Peace Corps. Hong Kong feng shui master John Choi told BBC in 2020 that because people are so competitive in his Chinese territory, luck offers a crucial boost for the rat-racers. Choi's argument explains why students around China might visit temples before taking exams that will determine whether they will rank among the lucky few out of millions of eighteen-year-olds with scores high enough for admission to the top universities. China's most prudent shopkeepers light firecrackers in front of their doorways, especially when first opening the business but also when starting a new lunar year, so they earn luck points that help them stand out against their many me-too competitors.

The term 'collective' gets thrown around a lot in interpreting Chinese culture. When it comes to demystifying superstition, it means Chinese people who believe they are lucky over a long period "might think that there is always a collective that they can work with to achieve their goals", scholars Ning Chen and Maia Young argue in a 2018 paper published by the *Journal of Cross-Cultural Psychology*. The collective can be their families or groups of friends but, notably, include ancestors and "other supernatural forces", the two scholars say. "Although their personal agency is limited, with the help from others, they are able to achieve successful outcomes," the paper says. Superstition happens to build links to the supernatural.

Placing fruits in front of spirit-world effigies at temples and launching pyrotechnics at the right times is supposed to please the supernatural forces. I lost plenty of sleep to fireworks exploding at 1:00 a.m. or 5:00 a.m. When I called the police one year to ask about the fireworks ban, an officer heard my foreigner's Chinese accent and said, hey, this is a Chinese city and get used to it. Ancestor worship is among the most common ways of seeking luck in China, with an estimated seventy percent practicing it. An altar to deceased grandparents and people further up the family tree appears in even small Chinese homes, some of which are built from the ground up with holes in a wall for urns and photos. I had a semicircular half-room altar in one of my flats in Taipei. The unwitting foreigner, I left it empty for two years.

Superstition appeals further to many in China because it allows for quick action on tough, long-term and puzzling problems. The actor in turn gets a welcome sense of control over the problem, whether it gets solved for good or not.

I know someone who wedges old towels under a centimeter-high doorway gap to keep cold air from entering her bedroom. The doorway is two rooms away from the bedroom, separated by a wide living room and a kitchen. The doorway leads to an enclosed balcony and contributes nothing to a chilly bedroom. I once raised questions and I got the blunt, angry answer that "I believe it works." The real answer: the towel setup offered a sense of control. To replace the leaky bedroom windows would have cost too much money.

Reasons someone might feel a lack of control: quality health insurance isn't universal, but disease is. University graduates compete viciously for well-paid, white-collar jobs in the world's largest talent pool, meaning a lot of others end up in lower-paid jobs. As noted in Chapter 24, getting those jobs doesn't follow a clear formula such as straight A's in college, but it's hard to know what the real formula is. Quite a few elders fear mishaps will strike again, regardless of their preparations, because accidents and illnesses were common when they were young and China was poorer. Someone they're close to might have died of disease before age 40. Who's the next victim feels all but random.

But fireworks are cheap and easy to get. It's okay to blow up a few Roman candles anytime the lunar calendar says a particular time, day or both are just right for improving one's luck. Visits to the nearest land-god temple in parts of China mean little more than a detour on the way home from work, yet they offer solutions that appear nowhere else. In Hong Kong, one temple lets visitors randomly pick bamboo sticks numbered from one to one hundred, each paired with a story that an on-site fortune teller interprets. The master's interpretation answers questions about job promotions and whether to rent a certain flat, both common but often answer-defying issues in daily life.

I had long wondered why formal education doesn't clash with faith in the supernatural, including ancestor worship. For an answer, I turned to scholar Anning Hu's 2016 paper published by the Chinese University of Hong Kong. Hu writes education helps build factually constructed knowledge about how to solve complex financial and health-safety problems. But a big slice of the educated population, plus many more, still follow superstition as a safety precaution in a vast, competitive society where the supernatural might suddenly become one's secret ally.

Why Authorities Get Blamed for Just About Everything

Go straight to the top, the thinking goes. Thousands of people from all over China once gathered with thick stacks of evidence outside a compound of low-rise brick buildings in gritty south Beijing for the chance to file grievances with the state. I interviewed dozens and wrote up the sadder stories for my news wire. They had brought complaint letters and thick packets of evidence to the compound, home of the central government's State Bureau for Letters and Calls, to ask for redress over cases involving confiscated property and police brutality in their distant hometowns. Across town and among the legal, architectural and advisory firms in Beijing's office district, drop-in visitors with business proposals were thinking the same thing: try first to speak to the CEO rather than the dozens of other staff people who are easier to find. Protests held in China, rare as they may be, almost always target leaders rather than appealing to society at large to make changes.

This targeting of the top reveals a widespread belief that senior leaders cause many of the core problems beyond one's own household and can resolve them all. The petitioners and protesters could just as easily point at developers, companies, mid-level government leaders or the education system for some of their issues. People with business proposals could file a form online with a potential partner firm rather than asking to meet the CEO.

Placing these powers at the top has its merits, of course. Ultimately the highest authorities have the most power to take actions and correct missteps. Disgruntled people in Western countries often write letters to an editor in-chief rather than an associate editor. They would contact a legislator rather than the legislator's aide.

But in China, this view of leadership offers a clear sense of order in an opaque world. China has historically quaked with political and economic chaos. Confucius suggested 2,000-plus years ago that people find their role in society so they can all live more predictably. Commoners for that reason typically expect leaders, who are toward the top of the social order, to handle higher-level affairs on their own, and well. Leaders tend to reinforce that idea by telling people they're totally in charge and relax—all's well. Authoritarian leadership at the national, corporate or even classroom level spotlights senior people all the more brightly. Leadership's failures incite outsized outbursts of rage in China because officials are so vaunted and so trusted to do so many things.

In the early years of communism, citizens expected their leaders to solve social issues because Mao Zedong's government created that impression. The Communist Party continues to cultivate a can-do-all impression now by monitoring everyday aspects of life, from the capital markets to the activities of foreign visitors. The Party still has a secretary in every school and every workplace. The state supervises the internet, too. Against that backdrop, it's hard to blame anyone for expecting the government to take full charge.

Ethnic Chinese people outside China expect top dividends from their own governments. In Taiwan, which has been ruled democratically since the 1980s, citizens figure leaders will prop up the free-market economy during downturns. Aside from stimulus checks and a bit of regulation, government agencies can't do much, because the market is boss. Taiwanese upset about economic malaise could question their own actions as consumers, workers and business operators, all part of the economy. But many traditional people there expect the government, given its high status, to reverse GDP contractions by itself.

Yet, perhaps ironically, leaders are not seen as common people's caretakers. The public usually gives leaders their space to fight wars and quell rebellions. Chinese leaders obsessed with fighting neighbors and rebels easily disappoint the public when they ignore for too long the problems that no single subject or household can solve, the likes of disease, air pollution and income inequality.

Domestic unrest helped bring down the Qing Dynasty in 1911. It had lost the Opium Wars in the 1800s, letting Britain force China to sign treaties and giving it Hong Kong from that time through 1997. The Qing went on to lose a Sino-Japanese war in 1895. Young Chinese were eventually sent to abroad to study Western thinking for clues about how the dynasty could repair its image at home, but instead they came back, believing the emperors to be corrupt and inept. The graft and failed wars had come at the expense of any concern for the impoverished masses' daily welfare. A more than three-fold population growth under Qing rule had left local magistrates too few resources to help people under their control. The Chinese public ultimately felt the Qing Dynasty had lost its 'Mandate of Heaven'.

Today's communists have reached deep into society to keep

people from becoming desperately poor and seething with rebel-like anger. Now the government seeks control over so many facets of life that just statistically something is bound to fail. Those rare protests almost always press a government, in or outside China, to right a wrong. Protesters in other countries challenge their governments, too, but they similarly demand that society as a whole change its ways, such as by eating less meat or being kinder to a racial minority.

The Beijing petitioners figured the Bureau for Letters and Calls could right any wrong via its legal authority over the counties, cities and urban districts that had sparked the grievances. "If I tell the central government, they'll tell the local government and correct the problems," one man who lost his home to a redevelopment project told me in one interview for the news wire. That confidence in the bureau motivated ruddy-faced farmers whose homes had been confiscated to await their hearing for days or weeks in biting dry winter winds. They stood alongside wealthy Beijing apartment owners who felt cheated by their developers. Petitioners from out of town even rented shacks along the nearby railway tracks until an officer inside the compound granted a hearing. A police officer at the compound gate once told me that the bureau sends most cases back to local authorities for a second review without passing its own judgment. Local officials in turn get even angrier with the petitioners, who make them look inept, dishonest or both. Outrage grows on the petitioner side, too, and quite a few justice seekers return to Beijing for another go at the bureau.

Some petitioners are years into their appeals. A few have gone to prison for protests. They keep at it because they hold the government responsible for their problems and just as capable of solving them.

Nature: Conquer it or Get Conquered

On a hike up a particularly popular forested mountainside near the southern city Guangzhou one day, I was stopped by a cluster of people. They were watching a woman hurl stones at a small reddish-brown snake that was crossing the path. Her aim was perfect, and the snake died from head trauma. Everyone moved on, satisfied, except me. My Western reptilian brain wanted to save the snake, which was harmlessly wriggling from one side of the path to the other. The two species hardly attract, but in China snakes are despised with extra intensity. Other wild animals, big thickets of plants, undeveloped land and other common manifestations of nature cause many people to quiver, too.

I found on casual hikes as well as reporting trips to Chinese farms a deep aversion to nature because wild animals, free-growing plants and imposing displays of geology are considered dangerous unless brought under control by humans. Human control means steady sources of food, shelter and habitable land, which were premiums in the poorer years before wealth began accumulating in the 1980s. Human alterations to nature, usually infrastructure, in turn, reduce threats such as getting lost or bitten by snakes.

Humans are a diverse species, of course. Quite a few, especially under 40-somethings from wealthier cities, enjoy hikes in the hills to get away from urban traffic and haze. Younger, educated, higher-income people such as my former students in Beijing are more likely to favor keeping nature away from human intervention. The US National Institute of Health agrees, according to a study it did in 2009. Chinese poets have reached fame by composing odes to rivers and mountains, while painters revealed scrolls depicting China's mountains in sensuous detail. China's predominant organized religion, Daoism, rejects notions that people can control other species.

But many among China's older, more traditional majority prefer knowing that humans have somehow harnessed the nature around them. Signs of control, and avoidance, are writ-obvious on public parkland. Trails, usually paved, pass multiple toilets, parking lots and stalls selling food on a stick. Landscapers plant flowering trees in formations, build artificial hills and carve creeks into the ground. Local governments lease parts of their parks to restaurants and teahouses. There might even be a bus ride from one side to another or a cable car cutting a swathe up any wooded hills. A walk through an urban park on the weekend can grow as thick with people as a stroll through the mall.

If you want a cardio workout, I was told, try the pool. It's safe, indoors and clear of water snakes.

For the poor, competitive and ambitious, it's easily smartest to use nature rather than let it sit. This outlook drives a squatter-like rush for resources, from harvesting plants in protected national forests to illegally hunting animals that can be chopped up and stewed. Farmers on the Loess plateau along the Yellow River have cultivated the land so intensively for so many thousands of years that it now lacks nutrients. The river itself, despite its moniker the 'Mother of China', has been so heavily drained for irrigation along its 5,464-kilometer course that downstream segments may dry up in the winter when rainfall is least likely.

A large number of elders in modern China once used land this way for survival. Few had the luxury of putting aside the search for food, fish, land and minerals to save the environment. Now a lot of them pass on this utilitarian view of nature to children who live in cities. That's why a pass through the park still beats a hike in the hills.

Naturally, China's eager builders, compared to their Western peers, meet fewer of the save-the-trees sort of protests when proposing to clear land for shopping malls, office high-rises and apartment towers. Urban sprawl throughout the country has chomped through farmland, drained rivers and spread across ranges of low mountains. Some mega cities have marched far enough to fuse with other cities that once stood apart—Beijing and the multimillion-person port city Tianjin that's technically 115 kilometers away, for example.

Fear of nature further motivates the quest to control it. Weather and bugs stand to hurt farmers and cause property losses. Snakes endanger people who lived off the land, hence, today's contempt. Farmers were once a more dominant class in China and older people remember those years. Fishing boat crews still grapple with the chill and high waves of the sea, prolonging fear of nature's randomness. It's hard to imagine surfing for fun near sharks and overnighting with just a plastic tent in the mountains hundreds of kilometers from the nearest town against the risks of being eaten or frozen.

As a suggestion for what to do in the wilderness, a recurring TV commercial once showed a middle-aged man walking into a bamboo grove. He took a nonchalant look at the sparkling green stalks and started hacking them down to build a shack. Then he tipped back an energy drink, the prize for his work and the product that the TV spot was selling. As a suggestion for what not to do in the wilderness, I cried out in defence of the next snake that I saw crossing a path and was threatened by human hikers. Five people looked at me like I should be stoned instead.

City denizens know now that rapid development and urbanization contribute to smog. Smog had grown so severe in Beijing by 2016 that technically cloudless days looked like they portended rain. The sun would peer through only as a red dot. Large numbers of Beijing dwellers would wear advanced facemasks, the kind that look like biochemical warfare preparations, to keep safe outdoors. They installed air filters in their apartments. But the same health-wary masses still, however quietly, accept the spread of development: infrastructure gets a generous new injection of government funding every year and developers keep applying for permits to build new highrises, all of which burn fuel and kick dust into the air. The new construction is still widely seen as a sign of China's progress, health worries aside.

As one shopkeeper in the soot-covered, coal belt city of Taiyuan told me when I was sent there to write a story on her city's air pollution, "We're just used to it. We grew up here." Just about everyone there had black fingertips from touching airborne coal dust that had settled on just about every surface down to the doorknobs.

Tourists are now spared memories of tough farming or fishing by taking in mountain scenery from a coach window rather than on foot. Cable cars eliminate the need for hikes uphill. To plod along the trails too long could conjure up sweaty memories of ancestors who worked on sultry, rainy farms because they couldn't make a living otherwise. At peaks in the national parks, visitors can be found crowding around pavilions that bear inscriptions about old legends and modern political heroism that took place there—signs of the human imprint on an otherwise unconquerable mountain. Hotels and restaurants occur more often than wilderness campgrounds in China's top nature reserves. There's air con. Snakes are rare.

Quiz for Foreigners: Are You a Good Fit in China?

Chinese people use the term 'Zhongguo tong' to describe foreigners who indicate they know anything from Shanghai's location on a map to every detail of the country's dynastic history over the past few thousand years, plus the Chinese language. 'Zhongguo' means China; 'tong' means 'passage or 'through', among other things.

If you're an outsider-wannabe-insider like me, take this quiz to find how well you get Chinese people and fit into their world.

1. How do you react when walking in a public park and you find a giant, dusty, noisy construction project has blocked the path, severing your communion with nature?
    - A. The park must be old and needing repairs. I'm happy to step aside today and come back for a nature experience some other time.
    - B. I don't know what the construction is all about, but it's sad people in this stressed-out city don't have more space to recreate.
    - C. Someone in power is using this public space to make money for himself and for his friends in the construction industry.

50 USEFUL TIPS ON CHINA

2. You step out of a railway station in a third-tier Chinese city and find multiple people staring straight at you because you're racially different.
    - A. You get angry, put a fist in the air and yell out not to stare. These people are mean and inconsiderate.
    - B. You roll your eyes and bolt toward the taxi queue to avoid so many gazes. China just doesn't get enough foreigners, you think, so they stare ad nauseum.
    - C. You put on a black cap so your hair color, if not already black, blends with the majority and smile at anyone who still stares. People are curious and well-meaning but all the attention is hard to take.

3. A Chinese colleague invites you to dinner at a ritzy restaurant. He does all the ordering, places food on your plate, buys more beer than you can handle and tries to pay. What to do?
    - A. Stop eating so your plate stays full and can't be stacked higher, send some of the unopened beers back and insist on splitting the bill. Let's just chat, you say.
    - B. Compete to fill his plate, out-drink him and pay the bill before he does.
    - C. Realize the colleague is being a typical Chinese host and would be offended if you resisted his food, drink and largesse. Treat him at a future meal.

4. The colleague in Question 3 keeps talking about politics over dinner, including perceptions that your country wronged China in the past when Chinese society was chaotic and the Chinese government weak. What do you say?
    - A. Tell him he has a one-sided opinion based on partial or inaccurate information spread by his communist leaders who don't want him to know the truth.

B. Reply with your own country's view on whatever he accuses it of doing.
C. Let him talk. If he's just repeating someone else's lines, however passionately, he will stop soon. Then remind him he voluntarily sat down for dinner with a citizen of the country that wronged China and see what he says.

5. Owners of the unit below yours in a Beijing apartment complex have moved in construction workers for a remodeling project. It's been going on for two weeks with no posted completion date. Drilling gets so loud you can't hear a phone call. Hammering starts at 7:00 a.m., half an hour before you normally wake up. What's your recourse?
    A. Complain to the building management. Remind them of rules for the whole complex that prohibit remodeling noise before 8:00 a.m. and require remodelers to post a work schedule in the foyer that includes a completion date. Shout at the management if they say they'll follow up for you but don't.
    B. Move out if you can't stand it. There's nothing else you can do but find a flat in a building that's not being noisily remodeled (until suddenly one day it is).
    C. Put up with the noise. Wear headphones. Everyone with money remodels. Someday it might be your turn and you'll want neighbors to tolerate it.

6. You're on a date with a Chinese university student. You've known each other about half a year, all casual so far but it may be leading somewhere. This extra special friend's mother will stop by the university where you're both studying to drop off some snacks for the week. You've never met Mom. Your reaction?

>A. Use the occasion to invite Mom and your friend to a meal. Say how much you value her child as a friend and that you would like to know the family better. Mom feels nervous, but it's your right to date and to treat people.
>
>B. Greet Mom but avoid introducing yourself or saying how you know the son or daughter. Mom would not want her child dating at school unless the two of you were serious about marriage, and then only after all the exams were aced.
>
>C. If you must be seen at all, introduce yourself with a business-like smile as a study buddy. Praise Mom's son or daughter as a hard-working student who will appreciate the snacks. Make a good impression for future use, in case the relationship gets more serious and you want Mom's approval for marriage.

7. You're in a shopping mall with a friend and see a Chinese man around age seventy-five walking through crowds of brash people with a hyperactive five-year-old who calls him 'Grandpa' and keeps yanking his arm to look at expensive toys. You comment to the friend:

>A. The poor guy is going to tire himself out taking care of a wild kid in such a crazy place. How could the kid's parents make the man go out like this?
>
>B. It's nice of Grandpa to take the child to a toy fantasyland,

but I hope he doesn't answer the kid's pressure to buy things. You don't want another spoiled only-child, and isn't he on a fixed income?

C. Grandpa probably looks forward to this outing more than anything in his weekly routine because family matters that much to him, plus, he's retired. He won't mind the crowds, the kid's hyperactivity or spending money on a toy.

8. A university graduate with marks averaging in the high 90s and a professor's recommendation is applying for a well-paid career job with a famous investment bank against someone with scores in the 70s and a recommendation from a friend in the company. Who gets hired?

    A. The graduate with scores in the 90s. The scores imply diligence and skillfulness. The professor's nod vouches for these qualities.
    B. All applicants will take an in-house skills test. Results of that test are more reliable than outside transcripts and recommendations. The top scorer gets hired.
    C. The graduate with scores in the 70s. An in-house connection supersedes scores, tests and outside recommendations.

9. You're a university lecturer in China and believe several students plagiarized their final papers because the written English looks native. Your reaction?

    A. Demand that everyone reveals the sources of all content on papers that lack attribution. Cross-check each source online. Fail anyone who plagiarizes.
    B. You'll never know exactly where anything comes from. Accept papers written with an original thesis and an

original conclusion.

C. Almost every academic paper is at least partly plagiarized. Chinese see copying as respect for the source, not as a violation. Give exams next semester instead of papers. Exams are normal and widely accepted in China.

10. A co-worker comes up to you one day and says she has a friend who's applying for admission to a graduate program in Canada and asks whether you could proofread the essay on her application. You want to help, but as native English speaker you've been asked this favor before and you're tiring of it. You've never met the applicant. How do you answer?

   A. Say "no" and lie that you're too busy or that you don't really know what the admissions committee is looking for.
   B. Agree to proofread the essay but make the task ultra-low priority. The longer your colleague's friend waits, the more she will realize she's imposing on your time.
   C. Proofread the essay that night after work. You'll be rewarded short and long term. The colleague will buy you lunch. When you need a favor in China, guess who will help?

Scoring the quiz:

Each 'A' answer gets two points; each 'B' gets three points and each 'C' gets five points.

Scores of 25 and lower: You're struggling to 'get' China.

Scores of 25-40: You're getting China but still see it through the eyes of a foreigner. I confess to a score in this range.

Scores of 40 and higher: Zhongguo tong! Get the T-shirt. But if anyone asks, politely deny the achievement and say you're still learning. That sort of modesty goes a long way in China.

Advisory: Drink Chinese Tea

Suppose that the quiz results in Chapter 50 show that more knowledge is needed to understand China. Here's an idea that worked for me:

People the world over like hot drinks. Westerners guzzle so much coffee that some measure their daily intake by the pot, not the cup. Tea is the staple for China. The country teems with different tea types: black, green, smoky, flower-scented. It comes in powder, thin leaves like pine needles and sometimes balls the size of BB pellets that expand in hot water. Chinese can drink the brew out of a tiny cup, a mug, a bowl or a water bottle. With so many choices here, even someone not initially keen on tea should find a buzz somewhere among all the choices.

Tea originated in China as a ritual offering before spreading as a food (to be chewed and swallowed, not imbibed) and as a type of medicine. The Han Dynasty about 2,000 years ago christened it as a drink and the Tang Dynasty that ended just after the year 900 AD popularized tea drinking as an art form. It was a particular hit among Buddhist monks who wanted the caffeine to stay awake during long meditation sessions. Tea grows today throughout south and central China. China's land mass supports enough different soil types and climate variants to yield more types of leaf than found in any geographically smaller other Asian countries.

The choices offered by China's tea can daunt an inexperienced consumer, but tough decision-making gets easier with expert advice. China's teashop staff people are there to help.

Most shopkeepers know tea and like sharing their knowledge. A back-and-forth about what kind of tea to buy easily turns to other topics. In the process, the shopper should learn a pile about China while feeling connected to a local person, someone who if not lugubriously friendly will be at least conversational enough to warm up the customer with a chat.

Exchanges with tea sellers diverge from other retail encounters because shoppers are expected to hang out a while and, in the good places at least, try two or three kinds of tea followed by a discussion about the flavours. Tea is seen culturally as a catalyst for conversation anyway, not just something for the quaff-and-go crowd. The shopkeeper could be male, female, nineteen years old or over sixty. Whatever the profile, this person often works alone, creating a thirst for conversation.

A lot of shops serve tea samples on a wooden table shaped like a wide tree trunk that was hewn off at human waist-level. A tea kettle with an electric heater, a clay teapot and set of tiny, almost toy-like clay teacups sit upon most tables. Cylindrical cups are for sniffing the aroma. The rest are for sipping. Once sniffed, the brewed tea gets poured into the sipping cups. A shopkeeper will demonstrate this process. In the larger shops, hundreds more cups, pots and other tea-ware festoon columns of shelves as high as the ceiling.

Chinese-language skill is an asset as English-fluent tea sellers are rare to none, but interpreters are welcome.

The consumer might start off by naming a broad category

of tea. Green teas are safe. They're relatively smooth, aromatic and often less caffeinated than other varieties. But green is a big category, so a helpful shopkeeper should explain the subtypes, such as flat-leafed longing from Hangzhou, zhuyeqing — a sharp-flavored tea that resembles pine needles — and the wispy, sometimes honey-scented leaves of the maofeng variety.

These terms often mean little to a tea newcomer, so that's where taste testing comes in. A taste doesn't obligate the tea tester to buy anything. Good teashops see it as marketing. Customers should get a cup or two's worth of whatever tea they pick out, up to two or three varieties per visit. I've gone away from these encounters before on a speedy caffeine buzz.

Points of note as the shopkeeper goes through the brewing process: water temperatures average between seventy and ninety degrees Celsius. The amounts of leaf to place in the pot vary from just covering the bottom to halfway full. Water may be added to the same pot of leaves two to eight times, depending on the type of tea, before a batch loses flavour. Shopkeepers usually start by washing the leaves by brewing them once and pouring off the water without serving it.

A customer is supposed to sip rather than chug the tea, regardless of the vessel used, which prolongs the tasting time. Here's where hosts discuss a brew's underlying flavours and the customer asks whether there's something perhaps not so heavily roasted and instead lets the honey scent come out, just for example. This chat could segue into a conversation about China via questions about where the tea in hand was grown. If it was grown in Zhejiang Province, a wealthy tea-growing region near Shanghai, the chat veers toward the province's sights and overall reputation among Chinese. An engaging shopkeeper will ask where a customer is from, an opener to extend the conversation. I've even exchanged phone numbers with the friendliest of sellers and met them off site for fun, chatter and more tea.

Where the chat goes next depends on personalities. Aggressive customers might dive into international politics and find passionate, patriotic responses on any issues involving China. A vendor I met in Guangzhou gave me a lecture in international politics, including China's history of immigration from Russia. Once in a while, foreigners meet someone who's leery of their own country instead. Cautious shopkeepers (the majority) usually restrict their remarks to life and the weather, and maybe socio-economic issues such as local job market conditions and the ever-rising costs of living. Whatever happens, the shopper suddenly knows more about China, and first hand.

Many Chinese people are curious about outsiders despite the sometimes bleak portrayals of foreigners in mass media and school textbooks. The shopkeeper's chat with a foreigner could help that vendor understand another country as much as it helps the foreigner grasp China. I fancied myself a scrappy de facto American ambassador in these cases.

Teashop exchanges, as lively as they may sound, often take just fifteen minutes, so there's no need to plan even part of a day around them. A teashop can be found in just about every urban neighborhood across the country. The writ-large Chinese character for 'tea' often appears above a shop's doorway or in a windowpane. Because so many vendors sell loose-leaf tea and because a lot of younger consumers prefer their tea processed and bottled, lines seldom form at teashops.

A sack of neighborhood teashop leaf should cost fifty to one hundred yuan. That price range buys enough to drink one smallish clay pot, with three or four refills apiece, every day for about a month. Larger bulk buys aren't recommended, because leaves eventually lose flavour from sitting around too long. Brittle tea has an earthy taste that's common among the courtesy tea served in down-market restaurants. But we're not talking about just tea. The shopping, tasting and talking experience at a teashop serves the newcomer a pot of China itself.

About The Author

Ralph Jennings lived for seven years in Beijing. He has worked as a news editor with the state-owned *China Daily* and an advice columnist for the 21st Century weekly in Beijing. Ralph ended his Beijing stint with the Japanese wire service Kyodo News. He taught writing courses at the Communication University of China part-time for nearly five years. These jobs exposed the author to thousands of news interviewees, media colleagues, students and their friends. Then came the random people who shared seats on overnight train rides, approached the author in parks and in one case threw a glass liquor bottle at him. They ranged from teenagers to retirees. He now lives in Hong Kong and covers the Chinese economy for the *South China Morning Post* newspaper and website.

www.ingramcontent.com/pod-product-compliance
Lightning Source LLC
LaVergne TN
LVHW030319070526
838199LV00069B/6506